W9-BGK-505

THE NATURE
AND THE STUDY
OF HISTORY

Henry Steele Commager

*With a Concluding Chapter Suggesting Methods
for Elementary and Secondary Teachers
by* **Raymond H. Muessig** *and* **Vincent R. Rogers**

CHARLES E. MERRILL PUBLISHING COMPANY
A Bell & Howell Company
Columbus, Ohio

International Standard Book Number: 0-675-09706-1 (Paper)
0-675-09707-X (Cloth)

Library of Congress Catalog Card Number: 65–21169

5 6 7 8 9/77 76 75 74 73 72 71 70

PRINTED IN THE UNITED STATES OF AMERICA

SOCIAL SCIENCE SEMINAR SERIES

Raymond H. Muessig and Vincent R. Rogers, Editors

THE VOLUMES AND THE AUTHORS

The Study of Anthropology, Pertti J. Pelto

Political Science: An Informal Overview, Francis J. Sorauf

Geography: Its Scope and Spirit, Jan O. M. Broek

Sociology: The Study of Man in Society, Caroline B. Rose

The Nature and the Study of History, Henry Steele Commager

Economics and Its Significance, Richard S. Martin and
    Reuben G. Miller

THE CONSULTANTS FOR THE SERIES

Anthropology, George D. Spindler

Political Science, Charles S. Hyneman

Geography, Jan O. M. Broek

Sociology, Arnold M. Rose

History, Henry Steele Commager

Economics, Kenneth E. Boulding

To

ALLAN NEVINS

with

Gratitude

Admiration

and

Affection

Social Science Seminar Series

Edited by Raymond H. Muessig
and Vincent R. Rogers

The Social Science Seminar Series is designed to present viewpoints about the nature and the problems of history, geography, political science, economics, sociology, and anthropology. The social science material is complemented by practical methods of study tailored to each of the fields, for both elementary and secondary school teachers.

One assumption of these six volumes is that the social studies program of our schools should reflect the social sciences from which it is derived. A second premise is that educators are responsible for translating social science material into learning experiences for the young. Clearly, the social scientists can discuss their disciplines only as they see them, and not in the light of how they are to be taught in the schools. It is the professional educator, experienced in coping with educational theories and practices, who must construct a framework to support the skills, attitudes, and appreciations drawn from social science. It is the educator, too, who should decide what can be taught at various grade levels and how the subject matter might be conveyed, buttressed and assessed by suitable methods, materials, and resources.

There is a critical need in all educational programs for up-to-date and stimulating material which presents recent thought in the social sciences. Teachers should see these disciplines as spheres of continuing scientific study rather than as static bodies of accumulated fact. They need, too, a more sophisticated grasp of the nature and interpretation of these fields as well as an understanding of the problems faced by those working in any given field. This Series is designed to assist teachers to re-examine their purposes in and approaches to the teaching of all particular subjects related to the larger disciplines.

With this perspective in mind, the editors of the Series suggested that each of the contributing social scientists ask himself what his field does contain that educators should teach to youngsters. Each author was asked to describe the nature of his field, to trace its history, to look at its methods and procedures, and to select what appeared to be fundamental ideas.

To each volume of the Series, the editors have added a chapter to accompany the discussions and analyses of the social scientists. The editors have not attempted to build some overarching theory of social studies education; rather they have concentrated on specific classroom methods. The concluding chapters in this Series, therefore, do not present either a total program or a master theory. The generalizations the editors have chosen to emphasize are not a basis for a course or a sequence of offerings; the ideas they have introduced transcend particular topics, themes, or programs. Nor have the editors attempted at this time to deal with *why, where,* and *when* questions regarding the place of particular social sciences in the social studies. As they see it, each social science can be taught by itself, woven into existing patterns for supplementary purposes, or assigned a place in some yet-to-be-developed curriculum design.

Limitations of space have not permitted exhaustive treatment of ideas drawn from each of the social sciences. Instead, the editors have submitted a variety of procedures that might be used, or adapted for use in a variety of situations. It is not intended that the ideas offered in the Series be employed in an isolated or disjointed fashion: a superficial flitting from one idea to another would have little meaning for students. The editors believe that large ideas should be approached and developed in different ways, at increased levels of complexity throughout the school years.

The Social Science Seminar Series is, we hope, a point of embarkation, an invitation to set sail on a voyage of discovery.

Preface

This book is the culmination of the cooperative efforts of an historian and two social studies educators. Dr. Henry Steele Commager, Professor of History and American Studies at Amherst College, wrote the first five chapters dealing directly with history as an academic discipline. Professor Commager discusses history's nature, purposes, goals, and insights, as well as its procedures and problems. Woven into Professor Commager's manuscript is a wealth of enriching sources for further reading and study.

The last chapter, on classroom methods, was written by Professor Raymond H. Muessig of the College of Education at The Ohio State University and Professor Vincent R. Rogers of the College of Education at the University of Minnesota. Focusing on a group of compelling ideas drawn from Professor Commager's preceding chapters, Professors Muessig and Rogers propose and illustrate numerous approaches teachers might employ to help elementary and secondary school students gain some understanding of these important historical observations.

The Editors

Table
of
Contents

Chapter 1 THE NATURE OF HISTORY, 1

Chapter 2 THE VARIETIES OF HISTORY, 15

Chapter 3 THE STUDY OF HISTORY, 27

Reading History, 27
Writing History, 37

Chapter 4 SOME PROBLEMS OF HISTORY, 43

Limitations on the Historian, 43
The Trouble with Facts, 48
Interpretation—and Bias, 53
Judgment in History, 60

Chapter 5 HISTORY AS LAW AND AS PHILOSOPHY, 72

The Use of History, 72
Causation in History, 79
Laws in History, 83
The Philosophy of History, 88

BIBLIOGRAPHY, 95

Chapter 6   SUGGESTED METHODS FOR TEACHERS,
by **Raymond H. Muessig** and **Vincent R.
Rogers,** 99

Historical Generalizations and Methodological
Illustrations, 100–154
Conclusion, 154

INDEX, 159

THE NATURE
AND THE STUDY
OF HISTORY

The Nature of History   chapter one

The first thing to be said about History is that the word itself is ambiguous. It means two quite distinct things. It means the past and all that happened in the past. It means, too, the record of the past—all that men have said and written of the past, or, in the succinct words of Jacob Burckhardt, "what one age finds worthy of note in another." Sometimes it is said that these two things are in fact much the same: that the past exists only in our record of it, or our awareness of it, and that without such a record, there would be no meaningful past at all. Thus the great Italian philosopher-historian, Benedetto Croce, asserted that all history was contemporary history. There is, as we shall see, a germ of truth here. But this view is not so much wrong as confused and, in a sense, perverse. The past is not dependent on us for its existence, but exists in its own right. It happened even though historians failed to record it, just as the tree fell in the forest even though no one was there to hear the sound of its fall. History does not suddenly spring to life when some historian gets around to discovering it or recording it. The historian who clears up some puzzle about the past, or who discovers new material and fills in some gap in our knowledge of the past, does not in fact create the past, though he may recreate it. What happened, happened independently of him, and the consequences of whatever happened ensued independently of him. James Madison's *Notes on the Federal Convention*, for example, was not published until 1836; only then were historians able to penetrate into the very chamber of the Convention, to know, and to explain, what had occurred. Yet what had happened at the Convention—what delegates had said, for example— had in fact happened, and had made history. The consequences of the debates in the Convention did not wait upon the publication of Madison's *Notes*.

But if the debates in the Federal Convention were history, so was Madison's *Notes*. Just as what happened at the Convention had consequences, so the publication of the *Notes* fifty years later had consequences. It clothed with flesh and blood the skeleton of formal resolutions and conclusions with which historians had previously solaced themselves, and inaugurated both a more realistic and a more nationalistic interpretation of the Constitution.

What this suggests is that the historian, by discovering some lost ingredients in the past, or by illuminating dark areas of the past, can in a real way re-make the past. History is *there*—there in the fact that it did occur; there, too, in the conscious or the unconscious memories of men. The memory can be jogged, the consciousness can be stimulated, the image of the past can be changed. When the historian does these things he makes history.

History, then, is the past. History is also the memory of the past. Needless to say it is with the second of these meanings that we are concerned.

Let us consider history as memory.

For a people to be without history, or to be ignorant of its history, is as for a man to be without memory—condemned forever to make the same discoveries that have been made in the past, invent the same techniques, wrestle with the same problems, commit the same errors; and condemned, too, to forfeit the rich pleasures of recollection. Indeed, just as it is difficult to imagine history without civilization, so it is difficult to imagine civilization without history. As Frederic Harrison has written:

> Suppose that all knowledge of the gradual steps of civilization, of the slow process of perfecting the arts of life and the natural sciences, were blotted out; suppose all memory of the efforts and struggles of earlier generations, and of the deeds of great men, were gone; all the landmarks of history; all that has distinguished each country, race, or city in past times from others; all notion of what man had done or could do; of his many failures, of his successes, of his hopes; suppose for a moment all the books, all the traditions, all the buildings of past ages to vanish off the face of the earth, and with them the institutions of society, all political forms, all principles of politics, all systems of thought, all daily customs, all familiar arts; suppose the most deep-rooted and sacred of all our institutions gone; suppose that the family and home, property, and justice were strange ideas without meaning; that all the customs which surround each of us from birth to death were blotted out; suppose a race of men whose minds, by a paralytic stroke of fate, had suddenly been

deadened to every recollection, to whom the whole world was new. Can we imagine a condition of such utter helplessness, confusion, and misery? (*The Meaning of History and Other Historical Pieces*, New York, 1914, p. 5.)

Clearly the concept of history set forth here embraces rather more than most historians would claim: the total record of the past—literature, law, art, architecture, social institutions, religion, philosophy, all indeed that lives in and through the memory of man. We need not embrace this imperial definition of History in order to agree that man without memory would be bewildered and bereft. But memory, as we all know, is fitful and phantasmagoric. History is organized memory, and the organization is all-important. As organized memory, history takes almost innumerable forms, serves almost innumerable purposes. Let us consider some of the forms which it assumes and some of the purposes which it serves.

First, and if not most important, then most elementary, history is a story. That was its original character, and that has continued to be its most distinctive character. If history forgets or neglects to tell a story, it will inevitably forfeit much of its appeal and much of its authority as well. With the *Iliad* and the *Odyssey* story-telling and history are so inextricably co-mingled that we do not to this day know whether to classify them as literature or as history; they are of course both. "The Father of History," Herodotus, had a story to tell—the struggle between the Greeks and the Persians—and he told it with immense verve. So, too, his great successor Thucydides, who gave us the story of the Peloponnesian War. Livy and Tacitus, the greatest of the Roman historians, were both superb story-tellers, as are most of the leading modern historians, Voltaire and Gibbon, Carlyle and Macaulay, Prescott and Motley and Parkman. For, as Lord Macaulay wrote, "the art of history is the art of narration, the art of interesting the affections and presenting pictures to the imagination . . . by skillful selection and disposition without indulging in the license of invention."

Here we come to the second quality of history. History is a story, to be sure, but it is not a made-up story; history draws on and excites the imagination, but it is not a flight of the imagination. It is a story of what happened in the past, or what the historian is able to recover and reconstruct of what actually happened. In short, history is a *record*. It collects and organizes such facts as are available and relevant, provides some kind of framework for them, and lays down the guidelines for the presentation. It supplies order, harmony, direction, for what might otherwise be a chaotic assemblage of miscellaneous facts.

There are, to be sure, serious limitations on the record, as well as on the ability of history to organize the record; we have to accept this without getting too disturbed about it. First, the record is, and is bound to be, fragmentary and incomplete. That is particularly true of the several thousand years of history before the invention of the printing press, and of the history of many of the peoples who even after the mid-fifteenth century knew not the art of Gutenberg—the American Indians, for example, or the peoples of Africa, whose history is largely unrecorded. For much of modern history the record appears to be more nearly complete—witness the miles of filing cabinets in the Pentagon and elsewhere, crammed with documents from the Second World War. Yet even here, needless to say, the record is incomplete. How can we know what happened, during the war years, to each of the more than twelve million Americans in uniform, to say nothing of the forty million or fifty million men and women of other countries who fought in the war? How can we know what happened to the hundreds of millions of civilians who were involved in the war, as participants, as victims, or as spectators? The record is incomplete for another reason: the limitations on the time, the energies, the intelligence, and the practical and technical resources of historians. No individual historian, not even the largest committee of historians, can read all those miles of documents, all the newspapers, all the personal records of the combatants of all the countries involved in the Second World War.

The record is not only irremediably incomplete, it is also lopsided and biased. How can it be otherwise? Much of it is wholly fortuitous. Our knowledge of the past depends pretty much on what happened to be preserved, and what happened to be preserved is only a minute part of the total record, minute and indiscriminate. Much of the record has perished by fire and sword—from the burning of the Alexandrian Library to the bombings of World War II; much of it has been destroyed by fanaticism, religious or national; much of it has simply been lost: thus of the forty volumes of Polybius' *Histories* only five survived, of the 142 books of Livy's *History of Rome* only thirty-five have survived! There is no logic here, no pattern; what has survived is largely a matter of luck.

Largely—but not wholly; for what has survived—or rather what has failed to survive—is also to some degree a matter of power. Justice Holmes used to say that Truth was the majority vote of that nation which could lick all others. History, too, is in part the verdict of the nation which licks others. Over the centuries history has been written by the victors, not the vanquished. It is the Romans who have written the history of the Punic wars, not the Carthagenians; the Christians who recorded the triumph of Christianity over paganism, not the pagans; the Spaniards who told the story of the conquests of Mexico and Peru, not the Aztecs and the Incas. One of the less amiable traits of victors, in the past, has been the deliberate destruction of enemy records and the silencing—often by death—of enemy historians.

The record which has come down to us, then, is not only fragmentary and selective, it is also biased. To be biased is as human as to err. Everyone knows that bias enters into even the simplest statement of events. No two stories of a family quarrel are ever alike; how should we expect that a score of accounts of the Battle of Gettysburg, or of the beginnings of the First World War, should be alike? History is, after all, not something which exists independently of man; it is something that comes to us filtered through the mind and the imagination of men.

Of all this, later, when we consider some of the problems of history.

History as a record consists of three states, or processes, usually so skillfully blended that they appear to be a single one. The first is the collection of what are thought to be relevant facts; but remember, what seems relevant to one person will appear irrelevant to another. The second is the organization of these facts into some coherent pattern; but remember, no two patterns are ever quite alike. The third is the interpretation of the facts and of the pattern; and certainly no two interpretations are ever quite alike. Now, all of these processes flow into each other. The practiced historian is not ordinarily conscious of these separate steps any more than a skillful baseball player is conscious of the separate steps that go into a decision to strike at a ball. It is impossible to collect the facts in the first place without some theory of relationships among them; after all, what are you looking for? It is impossible to organize them into a pattern without some theory that dictates the pattern. And it is impossible to interpret them except on the basis of the material that has been selected and the pattern that has been drawn.

Neither collection nor organization is entirely under the control of the individual historian who is, in fact, wholly dependent on others for the material which he uses. No individual scholar can go very far in the collection of his material; mostly it has been done for him, over the years and the centuries, by earlier scholars; by archivists who have preserved manuscripts and records; by devoted librarians who have assembled manuscripts and books, organized them, classified them, and protected them; by government officials who have provided for the preservation of court or legislative or diplomatic records; and by editors who have organized these. Imagine trying to write on the history of modern Parliament without Hansard's *Debates;* imagine trying to write on the American constitutional system without the 375 or so volumes of the Supreme Court *Reports,* to say nothing of the thousands of volumes of lower court decisions; imagine trying to reconstruct the history of the

French in Canada without the *Jesuit Relations;* imagine trying to interpret Thomas Jefferson without the help of—nay without total dependence on—the devoted editors who have collected his papers and made them available to other scholars.

It is interpretation—the third step in the organization of the record—which is most nearly individual and which therefore makes the highest demands upon the historian. Industry will go far towards solving the first problem, that of collecting the materials; common sense and judgment will contribute much to the second, the organization of the materials. But intelligence of a high order is required for the interpretation of the facts. The greatest of historians, certainly in modern times, have been the interpreters; and all the major modern historians have tried to be interpreters—that is they tried to extract some meaning out of the inchoate raw materials of history, or to impose some philosophy upon it. Thus the great English historians: Clarendon and Gibbon and Hume, Macaulay and Froude and Lecky, Buckle and Freeman, Maitland and Lord Acton, and in our own day Namier and Butterfield, and Father David Knowles and Veronica Wedgwood, and Denis Brogan and Winston Churchill. Thus in France, Montesquieu and Voltaire and Michelet and Taine and Tocqueville and Aulard; thus in Germany, Niebuhr and Ranke, and von Sybel and Treitschke and Lamprecht, and Burckhardt, and more recently, Meinecke and Rothfels. Thus in the United States Francis Parkman and John Lothrop Motley, Henry Adams and Vernon Parrington, Lawrence Gipson, S. E. Morison, and Allan Nevins.

Yet while interpretation depends on the accumulation of facts and their skillful organization, even the most prodigious industry and the most painstaking analysis do not guarantee a profound interpretation. That requires judgment, originality, imagination, and art. And this brings us to the third form, or character, of history—history as art. As Arthur Schlesinger, Jr., has said:

> All the elements of artistic form are as organic in historical as in any other kind of literary composition. There are limits on the historian's capacity for invention, but there need be none on his capacity for insight. Written history, after all, is the application of an aesthetic vision to a welter of facts; and both the weight and the vitality of an historical work depend on the quality of the vision. ("The Historian as Artist.")

This is another way of saying that history is a branch of literature and that it serves some of the purposes and is governed by some of the principles of literature. Certainly most of the historical writing which we call great, and put into the category of the "classics," has literary distinction.

Literary history is not just a matter of fine writing. That can easily be overdone, and often is; the best style is plain and straightforward, as with Lincoln or Churchill in the realm of politics, or Trevelyan and Brogan among English historians, Douglas Freeman and Allan Nevins among American. Literary style is a matter rather of the tone, the color, the movement of the narrative; it is a matter of symmetry of structure, concentration of effort, architectural unity and harmony, and the imagination which suffuses the whole. Listen to an example from a master of literary style who was also a master of historical fact, Francis Parkman, calling to our attention one of the paradoxes of Franco-American history:

> The French dominion is a memory of the past; and when we invoke its departed shades, they rise upon us from their graves in strange, romantic guise. Again their ghostly camp-fires seem to burn, and the fitful light is cast around on lord and vassal and black-robed priest, mingled with wild forms of savage warriors, knit in close fellowship on the same stern errand. A boundless vision grows upon us: an untamed continent; vast wastes of forest verdure; mountains silent in primeval sleep; river, lake, and glimmering pool; wilderness oceans mingling with the sky. Such was the domain which France conquered for civilization. Plumed helmets gleamed in the shades of its forests, priestly vestments in its dens and fastnesses of ancient barbarism. Men steeped in antique learning, pale with the close breath of the cloister, here spent the noon and evening of their lives, ruled savage hordes with a mild parental sway, and stood serene before the direst shapes of death. Men of courtly nurture, heirs to the polish of a far-reaching ancestry, here, with their dauntless hardihood put to shame the boldest sons of toil. (*Pioneers of France in the New World*, preface.)

While it is true that unless history is reasonably accurate and fair it should not be read, it is equally true that unless history is well written it will not be read. "The world at large," writes Allan Nevins, himself a distinguished practitioner of literary history,

> will sooner forgive lack of scientific solidity than lack of literary charm. The great preservative in history, as in all else, is style. A book of consummate literary art may abound in passages of bad history, but nevertheless carry generation after generation before it. It is useless to protest that Lord Clarendon was far too biased on the English Civil War; he will be read for centuries by all who savor a close-packed, pithy, eloquent style, full of graphic sketches of men and events. Motley is unscientific in his treatment of Spanish misrule in the Netherlands, but the world will continue to read Motley. If an historian were compelled to take his choice, fame might urge him to select the winged pen, rather than the Aristotelian mind, to choose Apollo against Minerva; but he may

choose both. (*The Gateway to History,* Garden City, N.Y.: Doubleday & Company, Inc., 1962 ed., p. 379.)

Justice Holmes used to say, finely, that "life is painting a picture, not doing a sum." So we may say that writing history is painting a picture, not taking a photograph. It is not enough to give photographic exactness; not even a photograph by Brady carries the impact of a painting by Goya, the "Massacre" for example. It is not enough to compile statistics; if it were, the *Statistical Abstract of the United States* would be, each year, our best historical volume. It is not enough to pile up mountains of historical and social details; if it were, the raw materials of newspapers would suffice for historical literature. It is not enough to put together strings of episodes and anecdotes, no matter how dramatic; picture magazines which do this dull rather than excite the mind. History must rest on statistics, embrace details, exploit drama, but it should control all of these ingredients as an artist controls the ingredients of his materials and the elements of his subject—control them, master them, penetrate them with meaning and suffuse them with imagination.

Yet we must keep ever in mind that literary history, or history as literature, is not merely a matter of style—the winged word, the happy phrase, the brilliant epigram, the dramatist's art. The historian does not enroll, automatically, in the literary school when he writes well, nor suffer expulsion from that school when he writes in a flat or wooden style. Literary history is something more than a matter of style; it is something more than a matter of emphasis; it is a matter of philosophy.

The literary historian is primarily interested in recreating the past. He is, in a sense, a painter, and who can deny a Rembrandt, a Goya, a Longhi or Canaletto, a Reynolds, a George Catlin a place among historians? He is, in a sense, a dramatist, and who would deny Shakespeare or Molière or Holberg the title of historian? The literary historian employs his talents to conjure up what was once real and is now no more, and to excite the imagination of the beholder to see the past through his eyes. Like the painter, or the dramatist, he seeks to capture, for a moment, a brilliant, a famous, an endearing scene, to recreate a picturesque tableau, to paint a familiar portrait. He is Motley admitting us to the bedside of the dying Philip II of Spain; he is Prescott making us spectators of the bold attack across the causeway on Montezuma's great city; he is Michelet bringing us to our knees as we look on the tragic scene of the burning of the Maid of Orleans; he is Carlyle involving us in the heat of the battle of Rossbach.

All this is a far cry from the more prosaic and realistic purposes of the scientific historian. The gap between the literary and the scientific is not stylistic; it is deeper and more fundamental, a difference in the philosophy of history itself. The scientific historian is not really interested in recreating the past for its own sake, nor at pains to stir the imagination of the reader; indeed he is rather inclined to distrust the picturesque or the dramatic and even the individual. It is reason he wants to excite, not imagination, and as for the past he does not want to recreate it but to explain it. A great "technical" historian—Frederic Maitland, for example, who "turned the dust of archives into gold," or a Hastings Rashdall who made the medieval university as familiar as the contemporary, or Father Knowles, or S. E. Morison, can write with a style that sings and soars. But their primary purpose is not to stir the imagination but to solve problems. Was the "Mirror of Justices," upon which Lord Coke relied, authentic? How did St. Bernard triumph over the Cluniacs? Why did the students of medieval Bologna and Padua organize into Nations? Were the Puritans really hostile to music and the arts? Each of our historians has illuminated these problems with literary grace, but it was the problem that was important, not the grace.

Let us see how two distinguished historians, one "literary," the other "scientific," deal with the same situation. Here is Van Wyck Brooks, of all historians of American literature the most evocative, conjuring up for us the image of Nathaniel Hawthorne confronted by the spectacle of the New England Puritan in Rome:

> Was Hawthorne right in feeling that "it needs the native air" to give a writer's work reality? Rome had provided him with a fairy setting for the last of his own romances,—the last he was ever to finish,—the tale of Hilda, Miriam and Donatello, the dusky Miriam of the shrouded past and the delicate wood-anemone of the Western forest. This dance of Yankee girls and fauns and spectres was like a Pompeiian fresco or something immobilized on a Grecian urn. A bituminous light suffused it, as of an afternoon in the realm of shades. One caught in the shifting groups the magical, mythological grace of Poussin. One heard Mignon's song rising from the depths in the fitful measure of a wind-harp. Hawthorne had drawn enchantment from the Roman air; and yet, for all the spell of *The Marble Faun,* it was hardly comparable with *The Scarlet Letter* or *The House of the Seven Gables.* The orchidaceous existence of most of the exiles seemed to bear him out in his distrust. One could dream forever in these Roman gardens, under the cypress and ilex, while all one's mental muscles atrophied. Norton, with his acute social conscience, his sense of a mission at home, probed under the surface of Italian life. The repressive political system disturbed him, and he had understood, from his own observation, the sorrows of Petrarch, Dante and Alfieri, who had mourned over their country and its degradation. Norton's critical faculties were alert; he had ridiculed the old romantic guide-books and the cold and pretentious work of the German painters who were dominant in modern

Rome. He had cared for the realities of Italian life, as Greenough and Margaret Fuller had cared before him. The others did not wish to care. It was to escape from the prose of existence that they had left America. If their writing lost all grip and bottom, was not this the reason and the explanation? (*The Flowering of New England,* New York: E. P. Dutton and Co., 1936, p. 477.)

Here is what Francis Matthiessen has to say in his brilliantly written interpretation of the *American Renaissance*:

The danger of Brooks' impressionism is even more marked in the half paragraph which . . . is the only space he has left for *The Marble Faun*. When he says that Rome had provided Hawthorne with 'a fairy setting,' and speaks of 'the dusky Miriam of the shrouded past, the delicate wood-anemone of the Western forest,' the flower that he envisages has nothing to do with Hawthorne's maturely bitter fruit. . . . As a result of letting his attention be deflected from the work itself, he has made one of our few major artists seem less male and robust, much less concerned with important issues, than he was. Of all Hawthorne's heroines, Miriam leaves a impression least like the fragility Brooks describes. . . . Her quick response to Kenyon's statue of Cleopatra (which is Hawthorne's response to Story's) is owing to her feeling within herself the operation of qualities equally fierce and turbulent. . . She is more deeply involved in a background of ambiguous guilt than any other of Hawthorne's characters; and his method of conveying this should be observed as a final aspect of his tragic technique, since it leads directly into the practice of James and Eliot. (*American Renaissance,* New York: Oxford University Press, 1941, p. 352.)

The differences here go to the very heart of the problem of the nature of history. Why does the literary historian want to salvage, to resurrect, to recreate, the past? It is because he is interested in the past for its own sake, interested in the drama, the spectacle, the pageant, interested in the actors and actresses. His is the view expounded by George Macaulay Trevelyan: "It is not man's evolution but his attainment that is the greatest lesson of the past and the highest theme of history."

The scientific historian is not interested in history for its own sake. He studies it because it is part of the evolutionary process, and it is that process which concerns him. He behaves, as Herbert Butterfield observes, "as though only those things are worthy of attention which gain importance from the fact that they led to something else." Like a good scientist, the technical historian wants to solve problems.

If the scientific historian has done much to illuminate the processes of history, it is the literary historian who has done most to expand its boundaries. For if we are to conjure up the past, not only its drama and its heroisms but its everyday simplicities, we cannot ignore the commonplace. To be sure, literary historians do yield to the seduction of the dramatic—witness a Prescott or a Motley, or, in our own time, a Guedalla or a Rowse. But Carlyle—who was himself irresistibly tempted by the dramatic—warned against this a century ago: "Mournful it is to behold what the business called 'History' in these so enlightened and illuminated times, still continues to be. Can you gather from it . . . any dimmest shadow of an answer to that great question: how men lived and had their being?, were it but economically, as what wages they got and what they bought with them?" Carlyle did try to tell this, and so did his contemporary, John R. Green; somewhat later, so did the Dane Troels-Lund and the German Karl Lamprecht and the Frenchman Eli Halévy, and so did the American John Bach McMaster, who wrote clumsily enough. But we conclude as we began: "literary" history is not a matter of fine writing; it is a matter of the center of intellectual and historical gravity.

History is art; history is also philosophy. Lord Bolingbroke put it for all time when, drawing on the ancients, he defined History as "philosophy teaching by examples." So almost all the great historians have thought, from Thucydides to Toynbee. History was philosophy in the Old Testament stories; it was philosophy in Thucydides, Polybius, Plutarch, Livy, and Tacitus among the ancients. Most modern historians accepted the Bolingbroke dictum as a matter of course: Montesquieu in his *Spirit of the Laws* and *The Grandeur and Decadence of Rome,* Voltaire in the *Age of Louis XIV,* Gibbon in *The Decline and Fall of the Roman Empire,* the Abbé Raynal in his many-volumed *History of the Indies,* designed, really, as an "instrument of war" against the Church and the Empire, and David Hume in his *History of England.* It is only recently that historians have attempted to discard this traditional function of history, and without much success. For philosophy, ousted from the front door, creeps back in through the side door. The public still wants philosophy with its history, and it is no accident that the most popular historians of our time—H. G. Wells and Winston Churchill and Arnold Toynbee, Georg Brandes and Oswald Spengler, Benedetto Croce and André Malraux, Salvadore de Madariaga and Raymond Aron, all wrote history as philosophy.

Yet few historians have been philosophers in any formal sense. They have relied on history, most of them, to teach simple moral lessons: the superiority of Christianity over other religions; the dangers of infidelity; the triumph of virtue over vice, or, in more sophisticated times, the futility of religious intolerance, the wickedness of kings, the depravity of man and the necessity of restraints upon his passions, the rise and fall of empires and the causes thereof—these and other lessons equally simple and equally dubious.

No one can seriously question the claim of history to be story, record, literature, and philosophy. What of her claim—or the claim of some of her more infatuated disciples—to be a science? History is invariably embraced in that loose term, "the social sciences," but we do not know what that term really means. Are the social sciences in fact sciences at all, or is the word "science" used here rather in its original sense as "knowledge"?

It was the Victorians who first asserted that history was a science; that generation, so confident of its ability to create a science of man, embraced within this concept the science of society, economy, politics, law, and history. Thomas Buckle was sure that he had reduced history to a science by bringing it under the dominion of "one glorious principle of universal and undeviating regularity"—the law of Nature; while across the Channel August Comte announced that "History has now been for the first time systematically considered, and has been found, like other phenomena, subject to invariable laws." And at the turn of the century two Regius Professors at Cambridge University, Lord Acton and J. B. Bury, intimated that if history was not yet a science it would inevitably become one. No modern Regius Professors now speak in such confident tones, yet the habit of thinking and speaking of history as a science is deeply engrained.

Clearly history is not a science in the sense that chemistry or biology are sciences. It cannot submit its data to scientific experiments; it cannot repeat its own experiments; it cannot control its materials. Wanting these, it will be said that of course history is not a science in any useful sense of the word. Yet it is equally clear that history uses or aspires to use the scientific method. That is, it tests all things which can be tested, and holds fast to what it finds to be true, in so far as it is able to make any findings at all. But how does history "test" things? What are the techniques of testing? How does it know when it has arrived at "truth" or even when it has achieved agreement of "facts"? The chemist does not inject his personality, his beliefs and prejudices, into the chemicals which he uses in his experiments; how does the historian rid his materials of such foreign ingredients? Indeed can the term "scientific method" ever mean the same thing in history that it means in the exact sciences?

Should it perhaps give place to a more realistic term such as "critical method," and should "scientific" history yield to "technical" history?

For there is this further, and sobering, consideration that the scientific method is valid—if at all—only in what might be called the formal and somewhat elementary realms of history, never in the really fundamental realms. Thus we can prove—scientifically if you will— that John Wilkes Booth did in fact shoot President Lincoln in Ford's Theater in Washington, on the night of the fourteenth of April, 1865. So far so good—but how far, and how good? For beyond that our science does not take us. Why did Booth do it? Who, or what, was responsible for his action? What were the consequences of the act? These, the really interesting questions, cannot be answered scientifically; they can hardly be answered at all.

Disillusioned with the claims of scientific history, some modern historians settled for what we may call Technical History—a term coined by Professor Herbert Butterfield of Cambridge University. Let us not aspire too high, let us not try to formulate laws of history, let us not try to don the mantle of science! Let us rather take problems, one by one, as a biologist or a philologist takes problems one by one, the smaller the better, and works them out. If enough historians work tirelessly at enough problems, we may in time obtain a firm foundation upon which future historians can somehow rear the grand fabric of history.

The stigmata of technical history are by now sufficiently familiar. It distrusts the dramatic and prefers to catch history in a chemical solution, as it were, in a moment of arrested development, and to analyze it and dissect it. It eschews the narrative and turns instead to Problems, though it does not really believe that any problems can be finally solved. It detests generalizations and is revolted by Laws; it delights in the minute and the specific, and its characteristic form is the monograph. It has little interest in ideas and none at all in individuals, looking upon them as aberrations from some norm to be arrived at by the study of statistics, or distractions from the consideration of impersonal institutions. It is impatient with the notion of history as literature and rejects out of hand the idea of history as philosophy. And it has an irresistible fascination for the academic mind.

In all this, technical history has obvious association with modern developments in literature, art, criticism, and philosophy. In the second and third quarters of the twentieth century, literature too turned from its traditional concern with the narrative and the dramatic to the analytical and the descriptive, abandoned interest in plot and in characters and entangled itself instead with the impersonal, the subconscious, and the amorphous. "Let us record the atoms as they fall upon the mind in the order in which they fall," wrote Virginia Woolf. "Let us trace the pattern, however disconnected and incoherent in appearance, which each sight or incident scores upon the consciousness." Art, too, became increasingly abstract and impersonal, disdaining to tell a story and reluctant to present anything dramatic, heroic, or colorful: historical paintings and portraiture declined with historical narratives and biographies. Criticism addressed itself increasingly to the explanation of texts, while philosophy turned away from the great problems with which it had traditionally been preoccupied to problems of semantics. In the circumstances it was not surprising that the historian, bemused by the intricacies of technical history, should look with suspicion on history in the grand manner—history as narrative, as philosophy, as art—and settle for something that seemed to offer intellectual security.

The Varieties of History   chapter two

There are as many kinds of history as there are historians, and each historian writes his own kind of history. And, as the historical philosopher Carl Becker observed, there are innumerable historians because every man is "his own historian." In one sense that is undoubtedly true, for everyone who tells a story recalling his childhood, or writes a letter describing a trip abroad or a baseball game or an exhibition is, after a fashion, an historian. He is doing, in a crude fashion, what professional historians do in a more sophisticated fashion; he is summoning up the past from whatever evidence is at hand, organizing his material, and dressing it up with drama and with art; he is even interpreting it all. And when he puts himself in the center of his story, he is giving us autobiography as well. Yet just as we do not describe everyone who writes a letter as a "writer," or everyone who draws a picture as an "artist," so we should not describe everyone who records some past experience as an "historian." We do well to reserve the term for those who consciously undertake to reconstruct and present some segment of the past, and who do so with some semblance of craftsmanship, for more than private entertainment.

How is history to be told? No two histories are ever precisely alike, any more than any two poems or novels are precisely alike; if they were we should call it plagiarism. Yet over the centuries historians have worked out a number of patterns and these have come to be conventional, just as have patterns in poetry, music, or art. They are not fixed, or binding; there is room for variation and for experimentation (suggested, in our own day, by the film and television), and there is nothing either final or authoritative about the familiar patterns. But on the whole it is the traditional patterns, products of centuries of experience, that provide the best vehicles for history. *of telling about history*

In a broad way these traditional patterns are the chronological, the geographical, the political, the cultural, the institutional, and the biographical. These are so familiar that they need little explanation or elaboration. The most elementary, and the most familiar, is the chronological, yet we speedily discover that even it presents problems. For where do you start? Start at the beginning, you may say, but that is not as easy as it sounds. There was a time, to be sure, when we could date the beginning with assurance: 4004 B.C., the date of the expulsion of Adam and Eve from the Garden of Eden. For centuries historians, as well as scientists, tried to fit their facts into this chronological straitjacket; not really until the eighteenth century did they find a way to extricate themselves from it. In the past century or so history has been able to move back a few hundred thousand years into something vaguely called Pre-history, and properly to understand pre-history requires a knowledge of anthropology, paleontology, archeology, and many other things which few historians possess. Yet something is to be said for beginning if not at the outermost limits of pre-history, then with the Magdalenians who flourished in western Europe some ten to fifteen thousand years ago and who not only fashioned implements out of bone but left us the famous wall paintings in the caves of Lascaux in France and Altamira in Spain. If we prefer to leave this to the anthropologists, we are still confronted with the question of whether we start with "civilized" man in Mesopotamia about 3500 B.C., or in the Indus Valley, which boasted an advanced urban civilization some twenty-five hundred years before Christ, or perhaps with the Shang Dynasty of northern China, whose people had by that time already evolved a written language which was to endure until our own day.

The conventional thing is to begin with Egypt, Judea, Greece, and Rome. Here, after all, we can find the roots of our own civilization. And here, too, we can feel secure, for the territory has been surveyed, the guidelines and signposts all laid out. And how painless the transition to medieval history, traditionally dated from something called the fall of the Roman Empire and the transfer of the capital from Rome to Constantinople. Oddly enough, even with the recognition of that transfer Byzantine history was generally neglected; historically the center of gravity may have shifted eastwards, but most historians preferred to linger in the West, though they sometimes fell into the habit of calling these centuries of history the Dark Ages. With an almost audible sigh of relief, the historian struggled out of the medieval era into the twelfth century Renaissance, and then into that glorious Renaissance of the fourteenth to sixteenth centuries. This brilliant era was the threshold to Modern History which could be dated from the discovery of the New World, or from Luther's famous Theses, as you wished. From then on the going was easy.

It was all far too simple, this division into ancient, medieval, and modern; indeed it was almost arbitrary. Its most obvious defect was its parochialism: these divisions did not really apply to history but to the history of the European West; they blandly ignored Asia, Africa, and the Americas, and assumed that nothing really counted except Europe, and that what was valid for Europe was valid for the rest of the globe.

There were other drawbacks. To apply names to long periods of history is to imprison them in our own concepts and expect them to live up to these names and concepts; we forget that the names themselves are arbitrary and parochial. People who lived in Periclean Athens did not think of themselves as living in "ancient" times, nor did the inhabitants of Tours or of London in the eighth century think of themselves as Medieval People. To apply names, too, is to generalize; it is to suggest, if not to assume, that all who lived in the era of the Renaissance partook of what we now conclude to be the character of that era; that the Renaissance Man was to be found alike in Florence, in Upsala, in the forest of Bohemia or the bogs of Ireland. Then there is the further difficulty that the designation and study of history by periods or eras tends to encourage the fallacious belief in sharp demarcations in history, and to blur the fact that eras of history blend and overlap just as the years blend and overlap in the lives of individuals.

Granted all this, there remains convenience. To study anything— literature or art, zoology or mathematics, we have to impose some kind of order upon it, divide it up and parcel it out. As long as we are aware of its limitations, the chronological order is as valid as any other and perhaps more convenient than any other. And may we not assert, too, that if we confine ourselves to a particular country—Britain or the United States—or to a coherent group of peoples and nations, there is much to be said for chronological distinctions? The Elizabethan Age, for all its connections with the past and the future, did have a character of its own, and so too did the Puritan era and the era of the Restoration. The Revolution did in fact divide the colonial era from the national, in American experience, and Czarist Russia differed sufficiently from Communist Russia that we are justified in distinguishing the two eras and studying them separately. We need not subscribe to the fallacies of the Zeitgeist philosophy to concede that youth and age have their distinct characteristics.

There is, of course, a very different chronological approach to history—to begin with the present, and work back. This method has its points, especially with the young. It is the way most youngsters find out about their family history: they begin with their parents and grandparents, and work back as far as information or rumor will take them. It is the way lawyers habitually work, from the present case to immediate and then to more remote precedents. Thus we can study such institutions as the political party, the Presidency, the corporation, the labor union, the university, by tracing them back from their current character and conduct to their origins.

We tend, most of us, to look with misgivings on the writing of contemporary history, and therefore on this approach to history. The information is not yet available, we say, or it is impossible to achieve perspective so necessary to objectivity. True enough. Yet it is proper to remember that many of the greatest historians of the past wrote contemporary history. Thucydides lived through that Peloponnesian War whose history he relates; Tacitus wrote the history of his own times. Machiavelli's *History of Florence* is contemporary history, and Francesco Guicciardini's great *History of Italy* entirely so. Clarendon's *History of the Rebellion* is in part autobiographical; if Voltaire's *Age of Louis XIV* was not precisely contemporary history, Voltaire did live through twenty years of the Sun-King's reign. And who that reads the splendid pages of Winston Churchill's *World Crisis* or his *History of the Second World War* can doubt that in the hands of a master contemporary history can still be great history.

The geographical, like the chronological, organization of history has a kind of elementary simplicity about it that has long been irresistible to school teachers and writers of textbooks. The nineteenth century used to think of history as something that concerned only the European world, that is Europe, the Mediterranean, and the Americas. There was, to be sure, some fragmentary attention to the Near East at the time of Hammurabi and his Code, or of the Moslem conquest of North Africa and of Spain, or during the era of the Crusades. From time to time the Orient would be smuggled in—now with the story of the Chinese discovery of gunpowder, now with Marco Polo, now with Clive in India or the opening of Japan by Matthew Perry, or the Boxer Rebellion— how illuminating that the uprising of Chinese against Europeans should be called a "rebellion." Africa, too, swam occasionally over the historical horizon—certainly when Europeans began to raid the hapless continent for slaves or to carve it up into colonies.

All of this represented a curious kind of historical astigmatism. Eighteenth century historians—Voltaire, for example, and the Abbé Raynal—had seemed to break away from this European parochialism and "survey mankind from China to Peru," but even their gestures were artificial; clearly they were interested in the non-European parts of the globe only insofar as these may have impinged upon Europe. Only recently have historians generally abandoned the notion that history was something that happened to or affected the European world, and acknowledged that the non-European two-thirds of the globe is as important as the European one-third. Even yet this re-appraisal of history is only partial and fitful. The history that is studied in the schools is still the history of Europe; the history that is read by the public is almost wholly European—a term which, of course, embraces both the Americas, and the British Commonwealth. This deeply engrained habit of looking at Asia and Africa—and sometimes even Spanish America—as mere appendages to Europe illuminates and explains many of the difficulties in international political and cultural relations today.

Here again, however, there is some logic in the tradition and the habit of the organization of history along geographical lines. It is not only convenient, it is helpful, to deal with the Mediterranean world as something of a unit, to deal with Europe as a unit, to deal with the Americas as units. The history of all peoples is interconnected, but geography and climate—the environment—determined the course of history quite as much as inheritance, and the historian may properly make environment his starting point, and accept it as his framework. There is danger here, to be sure: Henry Thomas Buckle *(The History of Civilization in England)* made geography not only the beginning but the whole of his interpretation of history, and failed spectacularly to make out a persuasive case. But if we use geography as an organizing device rather than as a philosophical explanation, we will find it useful.

A third method of organizing history, and one which derives in part from the geographical, is the political—a form of organization particularly endemic since the rise of nationalism. Thus we almost instinctively organize our materials into the history of Rome or of France, of the United States or of the Confederacy. Sometimes, for convenience, we combine groups of nations: the British Commonwealth, for example, or Latin America, or Central Europe, or Scandinavia. This political approach to history is, needless to say, almost wholly a product of modern history, for the nation-state is itself modern. Of all forms of historical writing the political is the most convenient and the most popular; almost all history is now studied in a political framework and that framework is even used, retroactively, to embrace the histories of peoples who flourished long before the rise of nationalism or the organization of the political state. The political approach to history is the most convenient because historical materials are customarily organized along national lines and by political and administrative departments—in the publications of government, of courts, in military and naval records, and so forth, and in the collection and organization of archive and library materials. It is convenient, too, because it makes relatively few demands upon the linguistic talents of scholars. It is popular because it appeals irresistibly to national pride, connects itself dramatically with the interest and the practical concern of readers, and with all that is most familiar, from stories in the nursery to studies in the school-room, from politics to patriotic festivals.

In the circumstances it is not surprising that most modern historians have accepted E. A. Freeman's dictum that "History is past politics, past politics present history." Whatever the inadequacies of the political view, it can be said that a habit of history—it is too much to call anything so nearly instinctive a philosophy—which has given us such literary monuments as Macaulay's *History of England,* Michelet's glowing *History of France,* Johann Müller's eloquent *History of the Swiss Confederation,* Peter Münch's voluminous *History of the Norwegian People,* Henry Adams' brilliant *History of the United States During the Administration of Jefferson and Madison,* more than justifies itself. Whatever the limitations of national history, historians can, and do, overcome them and even turn them to advantage. Whether history written without nationalist preconceptions, or outside the nationalist framework, can improve on national history remains to be seen.

The student should keep in mind that the political approach to history is fraught with danger. It inculcates a narrow and parochial view of history, and tempts both historian and student to indulge in chauvinistic patriotism. It reads back into the past the artificial divisions of modern nationalism, and exaggerates the role of politics and diplomacy at the expense of other elements in history. By pouring everything into the political crucible, it melts down the rich ores of culture, religion, social and economic institutions into a single slab distinguished only by the political impress which is stamped upon it.

A fourth form, or pattern, of history is the cultural. It is not easy to define Cultural History. It is the history of the mind and character of a people, of the major ideas which appeared to dominate a society or an age, of the institutions with which we associate the conduct and faith of men. Probably no other form of history makes greater demands upon the scholar; probably none is more fascinating when those demands are satisfied. The requirements of cultural history are not satisfied—as some misguided historians appear to suppose—by a naked record of what was written, or painted, or composed, or built by a society during a particular era: during these years Mozart and Beethoven were composing sonatas, during these Kant and Kierkegaard thought deep thoughts, during these Renoir and Manet developed Impressionism—that sort of thing! No, the cultural historian is called upon to know, understand, and explain the ideas and interests of a whole generation, sometimes in many different societies, and to trace their manifestations in the whole fabric of history. As ideas are almost always cosmopolitan, he is required to cut across the barriers of nation and language and perhaps even of time as well. You can tell the story of the disputed election of 1876 in wholly isolated terms, but you cannot do justice to the Centennial Exposition of 1876 without bringing in romanticism, science, art, industry, and a dozen other subjects as well. The cultural historian is required to know the history of many countries, to be familiar with art, literature, philosophy, and science, and to be wise enough to fuse all these into a synthesis.

This is not easy, for where political history has, or appears to have, a certain simplicity and clarity of outline, cultural history is sprawling, distracted, and amorphous What is it, after all? Is it anthropology, as in Frazer's famous *Golden Bough* or in Lewis Morgan's *Ancient Society*? Is it sociology as in the fourteen volumes on *Daily Life in the North in the Sixteenth Century* by the distinguished Danish historian, Troels-Lund, or in Charles Booth's monumental *Life and Labour in London*? Is it economics as in Rostovtzeff's *Economic History of Rome*? Is it religion as in Mandell Creighton's *History of the Popes* or the multi-volumed *History of the Papacy* by Ludwig von Pastor, or Anson Phelps Stokes' three immense volumes on *Church and State in the United States*? Is it art as in Jacob Burckhardt's *Renaissance in Italy* or Berenson's *Painters of the Northern Italian Renaissance* or Rewald's magisterial volumes on the *Impressionists* and the *Post-Impressionists*? Is it education, as in Rashdall's *History of Medieval Universities* or Sandys' *History of Classical Scholarship*? Is it law, as in Holdsworth's fifteen volumes on the *History of English Law* or Charles Warren's *Supreme Court in United States History*? Is it science as in Needham's *History of Science in China* or Lynn Thorndike's monumental *History of Magic and Experimental Science*? Is it military, even, as in Fortescue's *History of the British Army* or Oman's *History of the Peninsular Campaign* or Douglas Freeman's *R. E. Lee* and *Lee's Lieutenants*? Certainly it is literature, and cultural history has traditionally adopted literature as its most convenient vehicle: the examples here are too numerous to rehearse.

Some historians have been bold enough to try to put all of these things together, to provide a synthesis which embraces the whole thought and character of a society. Thus, for example, John Addington Symonds' seven volumes on the history of the *Renaissance in Italy*, thus Alfred Zimmern's luminous *Greek Commonwealth*, thus Paul Hazard's eloquent interpretation of *European Thought in the Eighteenth Century*, thus Werner Jaeger's magisterial study of Greek culture, *Paideia*, thus Vernon Parrington's controversial *Main Currents in American Thought*, which embraces almost every expression of thought except the philosophical.

All of these have in common an interest in ideas rather than in "events," and a resolution to cut across the barriers which divide politics, law, economics, society, philosophy, science, and art. These are admirable objectives, but they are difficult to realize. It is far easier to write a history of the Sherman Anti-Trust Act of 1890 than to trace the complex and elusive elements that explain German, English, and American Transcendentalism. But if the rigors and risks of intellectual history are great, so too are the rewards. It is gratifying to reflect that the writings of such cultural historians as Burkhardt, Symonds, Leslie Stephen, and Troels-Lund, now almost a century old, flourish with undiminished vigor and influence new generations.

The most interesting development in recent historical study has been the emergence of what we have come to call Cultural Anthropology—a study, or discipline—which has flourished especially in America. There are, to be sure, respectable antecedents: eighteenth century studies such as Voltaire's *History of the Morals and Customs of Nations* and Raynal's vast *History of the Indies* could both be classified as essays in cultural anthropology. So too could perhaps the greatest book ever written on America, Tocqueville's *Democracy in America* which, in a severely formal fashion, embraced most of the social and psychological characteristics now explored by the cultural anthropologists. Other nineteenth century cultural historians, too, borrowed heavily from anthropology: examples are Lewis Henry Morgan's pioneering *Ancient Society,* or Frazer's classic *Golden Bough,* or Wilhelm Grönbeck's neglected *Culture of the Teutons,* or Thorstein Veblen's epoch-making *Theory of the Leisure Class.* It is upon the work of such historians, and upon the writings of sociologists like Herbert Spencer and Lester Ward, that the new school of cultural anthropologists build. Perhaps their methods and techniques are more original than their ideas. To the highly civilized societies of America or Britain they apply the techniques originally developed for the study of primitive societies— the societies of Samoa or the Trobriand Islands or of the Pueblo Indians. With what they hope is scientific objectivity they turn their anthropological and sociological spotlights on the habits, customs, rites, and ceremonies of Middletown or Plainville, U.S.A., of Manchester, or Copenhagen, or the Vaucluse. They have little interest in the familiar subjects— politics or literature or philosophy or art—but address themselves rather to such matters as toilet training, dating patterns, the play and games of children, the sexual practices, eating habits, prestige concepts, and racial attitudes of adults.

Perhaps the chief value of all this to the historian was that it gave a new dimension to that familiar and traditional enterprise, the study of national character. The nineteenth century had been fascinated by this concept, and such books as Tocqueville's *Democracy in America* and Emerson's *English Traits* had given it respectability, while W. E. H. Lecky, the historian of eighteenth century Britain, had gone so far as to insist that national character was the only subject worthy of study. But as, increasingly, in the twentieth century, nationalism and race lent themselves willingly to the most evil purposes, historians became wary of generalization about national character, and eventually all but abandoned the notion that there was any such thing. After all, they said, men are more alike than they are different, and national traits are fortuitous rather than inherent; the whole idea of national character is romantic and probably pernicious.

Now, however, with the rise of the cultural anthropologists, the stone which the builders rejected became the cornerstone of the new history. As the historians hastened to abandon the field of cultural nationalism, the cultural anthropologists moved in. If there was no national character, there were national characteristics. Soon national character—and particularly the American character—was subjected to intensive statistical study by students of public opinion, child training, educational practices, class and caste, sports and games, popular culture and popular prejudices, language and idiom, and power struggles. And on the basis of their findings—so one of their spokesmen asserted—"the statistical prediction can safely be made that a hundred Americans will display certain defined characteristics more frequently than will a hundred Englishmen comparably distributed as to age, sex, social class, and vocation."

Cultural anthropology has a further contribution to make to history; it helps to democratize history. No one can deny that history is, and always has been, discriminatory and exclusive. It prefers to dwell with Monarchs rather than with their subjects, with Popes rather than rural vicars, with Generals rather than with privates, with Statesmen rather than civil servants, with Captains of Industry and Titans of Finance rather than workingmen and clerks. It delights in the spectacular, the dramatic, and the sensational—battles, crises, famines, natural catastrophes, heroic deeds, and foul crimes. The annals of the poor, we are assured, are short and simple; mostly they are non-existent.

As long as history depends on the written record, and the record that survives, all this is natural and almost inevitable, for the vast majority of mankind have left no records. The historian who wishes to find out how the great mass of plain people lived is forced to rely on such artifacts as happen to survive—tools, instruments, clothing, folk art and folk ballads, or on such records as have been made by churchmen or by officials—births, marriages, deaths, records of military service, the findings of courts, the statistics of the tax collector, and so forth; in modern times these miscellaneous records are supplemented by the newspaper. In the hands of skillful and imaginative historians like Troels-Lund who recreated *Daily Life in the North in the Sixteenth*

Century, or Ferdinand Gregorovius who traced the *History of the City of Rome in the Middle Ages,* such data come to life; but mostly historians have neglected them.

The cultural anthropologist is not, for the most part, interested in recreating the historical past, but the materials which he assembles and exploits do illuminate that past, for qualitatively, at least, his interests parallel those of the social historian. He is not concerned with the great and the powerful, the machinations of diplomats, the rhetoric of statesmen, the strategy of generals, except as these happen to illustrate popular traits. His interest is, by logical necessity, directed to the habits of play and courtship, of work and of worship, to family relationships, popular preferences in food and clothing, popular ideas of right and wrong. Because the commonplace generally has deep roots in the past, the data which the cultural anthropologist so carefully assembles from such miscellaneous sources becomes, sometimes retroactively, the data of history.

There is another form of history, one that parallels and contributes to all the others; history as biography. A large part of history has come down to us in the form of biography. Many of the most familiar stories of the Old Testament are biographical—the story of Joseph and his Brethren, for example, or of David and Naboth's Vineyard, or of Job. Plutarch was doubtless the greatest practitioner of history as biography, and his *Parallel Lives of the Greeks and the Romans,* as we know, deeply influenced the Founding Fathers. It was Thomas Carlyle who put the biographical theory of history most strongly:

> Universal history, the history of what man has accomplished in this world, is at bottom the History of the Great Men who have worked here. They were the leaders of men, these great ones, the modellers, patterns, and in a wide sense creators of whatsoever the general mass of men contrived to do or to attain. . . In all epochs of the world's history we shall find the Great Man to have been the indispensable saviour of his epoch;—the lightning, without which the fuel would never have burnt. (*On Heroes and Hero-Worship,* 1841, Lecture I.)

Though few modern historians have been willing to accept this extreme interpretation of the role of great men in history, many have written as if they would like to. English and American literature are peculiarly rich in biographies: Boswell's life of Dr. Johnson, for example, or Lockhart's many-volumed tribute to Sir Walter Scott, or James Anthony Froude's four volumes on Carlyle, or John Morley's solid monument to Gladstone and his slighter but more brilliant studies of Voltaire and Rousseau, or Winston Churchill's six volumes on his ancestor, the Duke of Marlborough, or George Macaulay Trevelyan's glowing story

of Garibaldi, while in American literature such books as Beveridge's
John Marshall, Douglas Freeman's *R. E. Lee,* Arthur Link's *Wilson,*
Leon Edel's *Henry James* come to mind. Now, all these biographies have
one thing in common: they are history as well as biography. They place
their subject against a rich and elaborate historical background, relate
him to the great historical ideas and events of his time, use him to
illuminate the history of an age. They all belong to what we may call
the Life and Times School, which contrasts sharply with the personal
and psychological school which we associate with such writers as Lytton
Strachey or Andre Maurois or the American, Gamaliel Bradford.

History never gets very far away from biography; even such austere
subjects as law or science are illuminated by the biographical approach.
Nothing, to be sure, quite comes up to Holdsworth's massive fifteen-
volume *History of English Law,* but it is impossible to understand even
the history of English law without knowing the men who made it and
pronounced it: Lord Coke, Blackstone, Mansfield, Bentham, Brougham,
Eldon, for example. It is even more futile to try to understand the history
of American constitutional law without taking into account the personalities of John Marshall and Joseph Story, Justice Field and Justice
Holmes, and it is no accident that American literature is particularly rich
in judicial biographies. And while specialists can approach the history
of science through the technical literature on that particular science,
for the layman it is the biographical approach that is most rewarding.
While the history of American science remains to be written, Americans
are fortunate in a handful of first-rate biographies: Lynde Wheeler's
Willard Gibbs, A. Hunter Dupree's *Asa Gray,* Brooke Hindle's *David
Rittenhouse,* Wallace Stegner's biography of Major Powell, *West of
the One Hundredth Meridian,* and Edwin Martin's *Thomas Jefferson,
Scientist.*

For reasons easy to sympathize with, biography has always been
the most popular form of history. It is pleasant to read, dramatic, and
colorful; it personalizes and simplifies complex problems; it illustrates
the promise of Longfellow's *Psalm of Life,* that

> Lives of great men all remind us,
> We can make our lives sublime,
> And, departing, leave behind us,
> Footprints on the sands of time.

It is for precisely these reasons that so many professional historians—
particularly those who practice "technical" history—look upon biography
with a deep suspicion. Nothing, said the great Lord Acton, "causes more
error and unfairness in man's view of history, than the interest which is

inspired by individual characters." And Lewis Namier, perhaps the most influential of modern British historians, insisted that the study of biography was a kind of historical kindergarten; the historian should not distract himself with the study of individual man, but address himself rather to those great forces of politics and the economy which determined the course of history or those great institutions where the influence of the individual was negligible.

Tackle any major problem in history and you will discover at once that you cannot understand it in isolation, but that you are involved in politics, international relations, science, technology, economics, psychology, and morals. If you want to understand James Fenimore Cooper's America you will find yourself inescapably involved in the history of romanticism, Indian ethnology, and the controversy over democracy, land laws and land policies, and a score of other matters. To understand the Supreme Court decisions in *Munn* versus *Illinois* requires some familiarity with the history of agriculture and of railroads in America, the politics of Supreme Court appointments, and the history of English as well as of American law. The fact is that men and women do not live in compartments labelled "politics" or "law" or "religion" or "economics"; they live in all of these simultaneously. The same people who write constitutions and draft laws also build houses, marry and raise families, work at machines, write books, go to church, and fight wars.

There is no danger of parochialism or of narrowness in history; properly studied each chapter of history opens out onto ever-new chapters. Nor can good history be neatly labelled and pigeon-holed. Is Parrington's *Main Currents in American Thought* history or literary criticism? Who cares? Where do you classify Leslie Stephen's *English Thought in the Eighteenth Century*? It is intellectual history; it is philosophy and theology as well. Turn to Morley's biographies of Voltaire and Diderot and Rousseau, and you are plunged into the very vortex of the most exciting intellectual controversies of modern times. If you wish to know Thomas Jefferson you are required to immerse yourself in all his interests: in politics and law, philosophy and religion, literature, art, and architecture, agriculture and gardening, history and natural history, anthropology and ethnology, education and libraries, and a dozen other things as well. History is as all-embracing as life itself and the mind of man.

The Study of History

chapter three

READING HISTORY

Does it make any difference what history we read? Justice Holmes once said that any subject is great when greatly pursued. A dull scholar can make even *Hamlet* or the Declaration of Independence dull, while a luminous mind like John Livingston Lowes can write a fascinating work, *The Road to Xanadu*, on the sources of Coleridge's poem, and a powerful mind like Walton Hamilton can write an original work on a single phrase of the Constitution—"commerce among the several states"—which throws new light on *The Power to Govern*. Admitting this, it still does make a difference what the scholar writes or the student reads. While, no doubt, all historical subjects are equal, some are more equal than others, and while all eras of history are interesting, as it turns out, the Renaissance, Elizabethan England, the French Revolution have a richness, a variety, a complexity which have excited students for generations, and that excitement has communicated itself in great literature.

This is, after all, the common sense of the matter. Doubtless every child is beautiful in the eyes of its mother, and we have on the authority of a hundred poets that every mistress is lovely in the eyes of her lover. The rest of the world, however, does not necessarily accept these verdicts, but abides by its own standards of beauty or virtue or interest. Certainly a biography of our old friends John Doe and Richard Roe is not as interesting as a biography of Abraham Lincoln or Robert E. Lee, and all the art in the world could not make it as interesting. No matter what genius an historian lavishes on a history of the Tariff of 1884, he cannot really make that subject as exciting as the history of the writing of the federal Constitution, nor is the history of Harrod's store, splendid as that London emporium doubtless is, quite in a class with the history of the Spanish Armada. It is no accident that almost all business biographies—purchased at no matter what cost—are failures, or that almost any book on Jefferson or Disraeli or Winston Churchill is interesting.

From this it follows that the argument for studying Periclean Athens or Renaissance Florence or the federal Constitution or the American Civil War is a circular one: for generations affluent minds have lavished their attention upon these and similar subjects, and the student can be sure, therefore, of a rich storehouse on which to draw. Just as we tend to study those areas of art which produced great artists—a Leonardo, a Raphael, a Michelangelo for example—or those chapters of the history of music which recount the careers of a Bach, a Haydn, a Mozart, a Beethoven, so we may be forgiven if we prefer to study those chapters of history which have produced or inspired the greatest historians.

For purposes of study, then, there are some preferred chapters of history. Study those chapters of history which, for one reason or another, have attracted first-rate minds and talents to their exposition. Study the history of ancient Greece because some of the greatest poets and dramatists and historians of all time recorded that history, and because for over two thousand years Greece has exercised an irresistible fascination over the minds of men. Study the Italian Renaissance because that study will take you to Florence, Siena, Rome, Milan, Venice, and because countless rich minds have been there before you and celebrated what they found: Cellini and Machiavelli and Castiglioni and Guicciardini, for example, among the contemporaries, and Jacob Burckhardt and John Addington Symonds and Ferdinand Schevill and Bernard Berenson among the moderns. Study the history of Puritanism or the making of the federal Constitution or the Jeffiersonian era because you will assure yourself of association with men of superior talents and characters, and because you will be guided, in turn, by historians who combine literary and scholarly talents of a high order. That cannot be said, for example, of the study of the Hayes or the Harrison or the Coolidge administrations.

A second rule for the study of history is equally elementary: read for pleasure and for intellectual excitement. History opens up new worlds, just as geological exploration and science open up new worlds. Needless to say history embraces both of these, so that through the pages of history we can share the excitement of discovery. The many volumes of the Hakluyt Society, in their enchanting light blue bindings, enable us to sail with Francis Drake and Martin Frobisher and Captain Cook to far quarters of the globe; through the pages of Beazley's great *Dawn of Modern Geography* we can share the excitement of the unfolding of the globe, the beginnings of cartography, the discovery of the compass and the astrolabe; with the greatest of all geographer-historians, Alexander von Humboldt, we can enter into a new *Kosmos*. Nowhere is the story of geographical discovery more exciting than in America; with Bernard De Voto we can follow *The Course of Empire* from Newfoundland to the Pacific; or we can concentrate on single chapters of that story by familiarizing ourselves with the exploits of the eccentric John Ledyard of Connecticut, or immersing ourselves in the *Journals* of the Lewis and Clark expedition. The history of science, still in its infancy, is no less exciting. Joseph Needham's volumes on *Science and Civilization in China*—Herbert Butterfield has called it the most important historical work of our generation—opens up new worlds to even the most sophisticated; and so does George Sarton's five-volume *Introduction to the History of Science*. If these seem too formidable there are fascinating interpretative studies such as Giedion's *Mechanization Takes Command,* or Loren Eiseley's brilliant recreation of *Darwin's Century* or Daniel Boorstin's *Lost World of Thomas Jefferson* or Lewis Mumford's critical *Technics and Civilization.*

History has depth as well as scope. It enables us to enter into the minds and characters of the great figures of the past with a degree of intimacy unimaginable for our own day or our own society. In this it is like compounding family history a thousand-fold; it permits us to know the pasts of other societies, even those which have been swept away by time such as the Etruscan, the Aztec, the Inca, the Viking. It plunges us into the most enthralling eras of human experience and enables us to know some of their greatest characters—a Leonardo, a Jefferson, a Goethe, a Lincoln—more intimately even than their friends and companions knew them. Through history we can follow them in their every deed and, through their letters, their journals and diaries— records rarely available in their own day—we can follow them almost in their every thought. This is one of the most gratifying of all rewards of history; perhaps only in great imaginative literature do we get anything comparable.

Every student of history can say to himself what Wordsworth said to Toussaint L'Ouverture—

> . . . thou hast great allies;
> Thy friends are exultations, agonies,
> And love, and man's unconquerable mind.

For history—and perhaps history alone—permits us to live with greatness.

The student of history can say, with Stephen Spender:

> I think continually of those who were truly great.
>
> .   .   .   .
>
> The names of those who in their lives fought for life,
> Who wore at their hearts the fire's centre.
> Born of the sun, they travelled a short while towards the sun,
> And left the vivid air signed with their honour.

It is important then, in studying history, that we choose great companions. We would not willingly fritter away our lives on dull people, and there is no reason why we should fritter away our intellectual energies on the dull and the trivial. Concentration on the trivial makes for pedantry or for superficiality. Concentrate, then, on what historians have found to be significant. To be sure, historians are not infallible; to be sure, an original mind can often find drama and significance in what has long been neglected or deemed of no consequence. After you have become familiar with some of the great epochs of history, and some of the leading historians, it is time to do a bit of exploring on your own.

3.   A third rule for reading history is to read systematically. Nothing is more time-consuming and, in the end, more surely calculated to consume interest as well, than to read miscellaneously and indiscriminately; that is like reading whatever magazine the air-line hostess happens to give us. In history, as in most matters, order, system, and discipline are essential. No one who flits from the piano to the violin to the flute without mastering any one of them will become a musician; no one who dabbles in French, German, Italian and Spanish without mastering one of them will become a linguist. The literature of history is almost infinitely voluminous: there are at least twenty thousand volumes dealing with the French Revolution and in all likelihood quite as many bearing on the American Civil War, and it requires the Folger Library of a quarter-million volumes to do justice to Shakespeare and his times. To "dip into" every era of history, or the history of every country, is to court lunacy.

What is wanted is system and seriousness. First, then, read solid works, not books made up of fluff and stuff. The butterfly technique—sipping at whatever is attractive—is the kind of self-indulgence which speedily leads to satiety. If you are interested in the American Civil War start with Douglas Freeman's four massive volumes on *R. E. Lee* and then go on to his three volumes on *Lee's Lieutenants*. By the time you have studied these, you should have a deep and ardent feeling for the War, and you should have too an awareness of having lived with a great man—and to have seen him through the eyes of another great man, Douglas Freeman. Then you can go on to other solid works— Allan Nevins' monumental *Ordeal of the Union,* for example, which carries you from the Compromise of 1850 to Appomattox in eight rich volumes, or Bruce Catton's dramatic recreation of life in the Union Army in his three volumes on the Army of the Potomac, or Sandburg's lyrical tribute to Lincoln—there are six sprawling volumes altogether. By then you will be able to appreciate Stephen Benet's epic poem, *John Brown's Body,* still in some ways the best evocation of the War. Historical novels, too, have a contribution to make, and there is no other chapter in our history that has attracted so many good novelists or inspired so many readable novels. You can immerse yourself in novels like De Forest's *Miss Ravenel's Conversion,* in Winston Churchill's *The Crisis,* or in more modern and more realistic recreations of the War like Evelyn Scott's *The Wave,* or McKinlay Kantor's *Andersonville.*

By this time you will perhaps have had your fill of secondary works and will want to turn to the sources themselves—the vast library of letters and diaries and memoirs bequeathed by participants, the lively accounts of journalists and travellers—not to mention the reports of the many artists—the immense mass of official papers and records, political, diplomatic, and military, far too voluminous for any one historian to master. To find your way through this labyrinth of source material would be a desperate task but for the happy fact that others have been there before you, have surveyed it and mapped it and marked out the paths.

You are not set adrift on a limitless sea of diplomacy: Owsley is there to guide you with his *King Cotton Diplomacy* and E. D. Adams with his two-volume study of *Great Britain and the American Civil War,* and a score of other scholars as well. You are not left to wander aimlessly through the records of the battle of Gettysburg; a dozen biographers, a score of military historians, are ready to provide guidance. You are not left to conjure up for yourself the causes for the defeat of the Confederacy; a hundred scholars have speculated on just that question, a hundred books provide not only the theories and explanations but notes and references which direct you to the source material and enable you to arrive at your own conclusions.

Or suppose it is Thomas Jefferson who has caught your fancy— there is no one more rewarding, no one who better fulfills the promises he holds out on first acquaintance. The literature here, too, is immense, and you will do well to begin with one of the many good biographies— that by the French-American scholar, Gilbert Chinard, for example, or the three fascinating volumes by Marie Kimball, or the still incomplete biography by Dumas Malone. Once you know what most interests you in Jefferson you will want to turn to his own astonishingly voluminous writings. There are two older editions of the writings, and one magnificent edition still under way—some seventeen volumes published—edited by the greatest of Jefferson scholars, Julian Boyd. Now you will be ready for some of the almost innumerable monographs dealing with particular aspects of the life of this versatile genius. There is, for example, Karl Lehmann's wide-ranging essay on *Thomas Jefferson, American Humanist,* or James Bryant Conant's lectures on *Jefferson and the Development of American Education,* or Edwin Martin's fascinating study of *Thomas Jefferson, Scientist,* or Fiske Kimball's authoritative book on *Thomas Jefferson, Architect,* or Edward Dumbauld's delightful *Thomas Jefferson, American Tourist.* If you want politics, there are the volumes which the incomparable Henry Adams devoted to Jefferson in his *History,* or the two volumes by the diplomat-historian Claude Bowers, *Jefferson and Hamilton* and *Jefferson in Power,* or C. M. Wiltse's *Jeffersonian Tradition in American Politics.* Charles A. Beard has investigated the *Economic Origins of Jeffersonian Democracy;* Leonard White has done a definitive job on the administrative side of the Jeffersonian years, *The Jeffersonians;* and Merril Petersen has traced the *Jeffersonian Image in the American Mind.*

But this is, in a sense, only the beginning. You cannot understand Jefferson in a vacuum; you must know his associates and disciples, you must know his intellectual companions and his philosophical antecedents; happily these are well worth knowing. James Madison was, for almost fifty years, Jefferson's disciple and friend—the friendship has been explored by Adrienne Koch in a book on the two men. You will want to read Irving Brant's six-volume biography of Madison and to read some of Madison's own essays and letters in the older edition by Gaillard Hunt or in the new edition of the *Papers* now under way. Albert Gallatin, too—the Swiss *philosophe* who cast in his lot with America and became, in time, Jefferson's Secretary of the Treasury—was a member of the Jeffersonian circle: you can read his life in a masterly biography by Henry Adams, and his *Writings* are edited, in three stout volumes, also by Adams. You can scarcely think of Jefferson without his life-long friend—and sometime antagonist—John Adams: they worked together for fifty years and died, dramatically, on the same day, precisely fifty years after the Declaration of Independence. To know Adams is almost as big a task, and almost as interesting, as knowing Jefferson. There are good biographies by Gilbert Chinard and Page Smith; there is an admirable study of Adams' political thought by Edward Handler, and Zoltan Haraszti has set forth his relation to the French *philosophes* in the ingenious *John Adams and the Prophets of Progress.* You will of course want to read Adams himself: the *Diary* and

Autobiography have already been republished, in four sumptuous volumes, and the correspondence and miscellaneous writings will soon be available in the new edition of the Adams papers edited by Lyman Butterfield. But to know Jefferson you must know not only his associates, but his intellectual and philosophical antecedents. Turn then to the five-volume catalogue of his wonderful library which Miss Millicent Sowerby has edited; to the elaborate annotations in Boyd's edition of the *Papers;* to the many monographs on Jefferson's French associates by Gilbert Chinard; and to studies of the Enlightenment by John Morley, Carl Becker, Ernst Cassirer, Paul Hazard, Basil Willey, and a score of other interpreters. By now you will realize that to do justice to Jefferson is the work not of a year but of a lifetime, but that is true of almost every really great or spacious subject.

A fourth rule in the study of history is always to work from the particular to the general, never from the general to the particular. General works—outlines of this or that, surveys of everything—are almost guaranteed to rot the brain. The method of history is the method of science—inductive, and empirical; it is the method of law—the case study; it is the method even of art—to start with the study of anatomy, with the mastery of paints, or of stone. Begin, then, with the particular—with an individual or an episode or an institution—and work from there to more general subjects. Are you interested in the United States Constitution? Start with the document itself, read the debates in the Federal Convention (they have been admirably edited by Max Farrand) and the debates in the ratifying conventions as well, the so-called *Elliot's Debates.* Read and re-read *The Federalist* papers, incomparably the most profound commentary on political philosophy and on constitutionalism written in this country: there are several good modern editions. Now you are ready to go on to constitutional history. A good book of documents will give you many of the essential laws, proclamations, presidential addresses, and judicial opinions. A good history of the Supreme Court—that by Charles Warren, though by now out of date, is unquestionably the best—and a few biographies such as Beveridge's voluminous *Marshall,* or Charles Fairman's *Justice Miller* or Alpheus Mason's *Chief Justice Stone* or Max Lerner's edition of the *Mind and Faith of Justice Holmes* will go a long way towards clarifying the intricacies and complexities of the constitutional system. Genuine scholarship would of course require that you immerse yourself in the decisions of the Supreme Court—the very stuff and substance of our constitutional law and history; there are some 375 volumes of these, and here you will clearly need expert guidance; fortunately, a score of case-books which bring together the leading decisions are at hand. By the time you have studied the Constitution and the Court intensively you will have familiarized yourself not only with the American constitutional system, but with most of the issues of American politics, economy, and society.

The average reader, it is fair to say, gets his sense of the past not through the writings of formal historians, but through the pages of fiction directly or, in recent times, translated into films and television dramas. This is natural enough; the story comes before history in the life of the race, as in the lives of individuals. Biblical stories came before Josephus' *History of the Jews,* and the *Iliad* and the *Odyssey* before either Herodotus or Thucydides, and it is not only children who have learned the history of England from the stories of King Arthur and his knights of the Round Table, or from Froissart or Chaucer, but their parents as well. Winston Churchill (who himself wrote an historical novel) said that he learned all of his English history from the plays of Shakespeare, and Francis Parkman's debt to Cooper's *Leatherstocking Tales* is notorious, while G. M. Trevelyan has paid handsome tribute to the influence of Walter Scott on his own historical writing. "Fiction is truth's elder sister," wrote Rudyard Kipling, with pardonable exaggeration. No one in the world knew what truth was till someone had told a story. So it is the oldest of the arts, the mother of history, biography, philosophy, and, of course, "politics."

Cooper and Scott, and Kipling, too, remind us that the historical novel is very much a nineteenth century invention. It began—there were of course antecedents—with Walter Scott and John Galt in Scotland, with Fenimore Cooper and William Gilmore Simms in America, with B. S. Ingemann in Denmark and Victor Hugo in France and Alessandro Manzoni in Italy. These were, for a generation and more, the most widely read of modern writers, providing the whole civilized world with stereotypes of historical characters and episodes. The historical novel spread from England throughout Europe, and became a standard expression of historical nationalism. Almost every major writer tried his hand at it: Thackeray and Bulwer-Lytton and George Eliot and Disraeli and even Dickens in England; Victor Hugo and Stendhal and Dumas and Flaubert in France; Gustav Freytag in Germany; Sienkiewicz in Poland; Manzoni in Italy; Pushkin, Turgenev, and Tolstoy in Russia; and in Spain Perez Galdos whose *Episodios Nacionales* filled no fewer than forty-six volumes.

Nowhere did the historical novel flourish more vigorously than in the United States. Almost all the major writers turned to history for their material: Irving, who was both an historian and a novelist, and his friend James Kirke Paulding, Cooper and Hawthorne and the almost forgotten De Forest and the prolific E. Marion Crawford, and the southerners Beverley Tucker and John Pendleton Kennedy and William Gilmore Simms; even the historians Motley and Parkman managed to squeeze in one historical novel apiece. Harriet Beecher Stowe gave us *The Minister's Wooing* and many other historical panels, and Howells did not fail to conjure up frontier Ohio, and Mark Twain, whom we do not ordinarily remember as an historical novelist, produced *The Prince and the Pauper* and *A Connecticut Yankee in King Arthur's Court*. One trait almost all of these had in common—as did most of the English historical novelists from Thackeray to Stevenson—is that they wrote for children, or wrote books which children took over and made their own. Teachers and scholars too commonly ignore the needs of children, forgetting that if they are to be attracted to the study of history their interests must be aroused and their sympathies enlisted, and forgetting that children want action, drama, adventure, heroes, and villains. These the historical novel offers them.

There are, in a broad way, two kinds of historical novels. There is the "costume piece"—the novel which quite deliberately seeks to re-create the past and to dramatize it; like a producer putting on an Elizabethan play, the author has to be sure to get all the "furniture" right—the clothing, the idiom, even the accent. Traditionally this kind of historical novel distorts history, leaving with the reader the impression that the past was a potpourri of fighting, derring-do, and non-stop romances by Scott or Dumas or Stevenson or John Buchan. But at its best this kind of historical fiction can be as faithful to history as a good many sober monographs, and can be, at the same time, great literature: Thackeray's *The Virginians*, Hawthorne's *Scarlet Letter*, Stendhal's *Charterhouse of Parma*, Tolstoy's *War and Peace*, Sigrid Undset's *Kristin Lavransdatter*, Thomas Mann's *Joseph and his Brethren*, and Lion Feuchtwanger's *Jew Süss* come readily to mind.

There is another and even more valuable genre of historical novel—the novel that is not deliberately "historical" at all, but that faithfully recreates a present which is or will be past, and which becomes, therefore, by virtue of its authenticity, an historical document. If we want to know what life was like in the comfortable upper classes of England during the Napoleonic wars we cannot do better than turn to the novels of Jane Austen—*Pride and Prejudice* or *Sense and Sensibility* or *Mansfield Park*. Is there anywhere a more faithful picture of Scotland during these same years than can be read in the salty pages of John Galt's *Annals of the Parish* or *The Entail*—unless it is possibly in the pages of Galt's contemporary, Susan Ferrier? Has anyone ever conjured up life in the London of the early nineteenth century more realistically than Dickens in *Nicholas Nickleby* or *Oliver Twist* or *Great Expectations*? What better way is there to understand the bourgeoisie of the Hansa towns than through Thomas Mann's *Buddenbrooks*, or of French provincial towns than in the pages of *Madame Bovary*? Selma Lagerlöv has given us eighteenth century Sweden in the marvellously picaresque *Saga of*

Gösta Berling and nineteenth century Sweden in *Jerusalem;* and Bjørnsen has done the same for Norway. Louis Couperus helps us to understand life in the crowded cities of modern Holland, and if we turn to Denmark we have no better guide than Martin Andersen-Nexö whose *Pelle the Conqueror* and *Ditte Girl Alive* recreate Copenhagen as Dickens recreated London. No sociological treatises conjure up life in the provincial towns of industrial England more faithfully than Arnold Bennett's Five Towns stories—*Clayhanger* and *Old Wives' Tale* and others; no historian of the class system illuminates it better than do Galsworthy in the *Forsyte Saga* or Frank Swinnerton in *Shops and Houses* or Virginia Woolf in *Day and Night*. Americans, too, can read their social history in works of fiction. William Dean Howells has some claim to be regarded as our most finished and comprehensive social historian, Howells who gives us the placid life of Boston and of the hinterland of New England, the Vermont countryside, the Ohio frontier and the turbulent life of New York City, and of the American abroad, and whose *Rise of Silas Lapham* is still in many ways the best portrayal of the American businessman in our literature. So it is with a host of others: the incomparable Henry James, foremost historian of the manners of the American leisure class and of the American expatriate, and most penetrating student of the American moral character; Edith Wharton with her sensitive feeling for the life of the upper classes of New York City and the Hudson Valley; Ellen Glasgow, who understood so fully what had happened to Virginia "after the War," and who explained it in a long series of novels carrying the history of Virginia from the Civil War to the twentieth century; Willa Cather, whose panels of life on the plains—*My Ántonia* and *O Pioneers* and *The Song of the Lark* and, best of all, *A Lost Lady*—are more realistic and penetrating than her formal historical novels. For a feeling of life on the farm in the years after the Civil War, and of the truth of the farm problem, we turn with confidence to Hamlin Garland's *Main Traveled Roads* or to Frank Norris' *The Octopus* or to Ole Rølvaag's wonderfully evocative *Giants in the Earth,* rather than to the formal histories; and the most penetrating accounts of the "revolt from the village" are, beyond doubt, such books as Sherwood Anderson's *Winesburg, Ohio* or Edgar Lee Masters' *Spoon River Anthology* or Sinclair Lewis' *Main Street.*

These observations apply with equal force to poetry and drama. Lord Tennyson's *Idylls of the King* and the plays of Hendrik Ibsen are historical documents of the first order; read with insight and with sympathy they will illuminate the Victorian mind, or the social history of Norway, as brightly as any formal historical treatises on these subjects.

WRITING HISTORY

So much for reading. What of the writing of history? ⸮

Let it be said at once that there is no mystery about writing history, nothing esoteric or cabalistic. There is no formula for historical writing. There are no special techniques or special requirements, except the technique of writing clearly and the requirements of honesty and common sense. It is useful to have special training, as it is useful to have special training for almost anything you wish to do well—driving a car, or cooking, or painting—but special training is by no means essential, and most of the great historians have been innocent of formal training. Professional history is, indeed, a very recent affair—it came in with "technical history" in the nineteenth century— and, except in Germany, the near-monopoly of historical writing by academicians is even more recent. Almost all the great historians of the past were men involved in one way or another in public affairs—Thucydides, Livy, Tacitus, Plutarch and, in modern times, Bolingbroke, Voltaire, Hume, Macaulay, Bancroft, Guizot, Grundtvig. Most of them, too, were amateurs, at least in the sense that they were not professional teachers: thus in the United States Bancroft, Prescott, Motley, Parkman, and Henry Adams. The amateur tradition is now almost a thing of the past, but it lingers on in Europe more tenaciously than in America: witness the contributions of such public figures as Croce, Madariaga, Malraux, De Gaulle, George Lukacs, and Winston Churchill.

Integrity, industry, imagination, and common sense—these are the important, indeed the essential, requirements. They are by no means familiar commonplace qualities. The requirement of integrity is of course implacable, in history as in all other forms of scholarship or science, and there is no need to elaborate upon it. Yet here, too, it must be admitted that standards of "integrity" are not universal, and that honest men differ on the nature of truth in history as in all other realms of thought. Perhaps it is sufficient to say that the historian must be honest according to his lights; that he should never consciously distort his evidence, even by literary artistry; that he should be ever on guard against religious, racial, class or national preconceptions; that he should try to see every problem from all possible points of view; that he should search diligently for all the evidence, and not be content until he has exhausted the available resources; that he should always remember that he is not God and that final judgment is not entrusted to him.

The requirement of industry, too, is elementary and rigorous. You need not, perhaps, emulate the great historian of ancient Rome, Theodore

Mommsen, who customarily worked eighteen hours a day and complained that on his wedding day he managed only twelve hours work, or that other German phenomenon, Leopold von Ranke, who kept working and writing well into his eighties, and who at the age of eighty-five launched a *History of the World,* seven volumes of which appeared in the next five years of his life. But, as with most things that are important, the writing of history requires patience, devotion, and indefatigable industry, much of it tiresome. You will have to accustom yourself to spending long hours and days tracking down some source which as often as not will prove quite useless, reading through newspapers or journals which as often as not yield only a scanty return, working patiently through ill-scrawled manuscripts in the hope, often vain, of hitting on something that is relevant to your inquiry, fighting your way stubbornly through the jungles of verbiage in the *Congressional Globe* or the *Reports* of royal commissions, or the decisions of courts. If you are going to come up with something that is new, original, fresh, and valuable, you cannot avoid these exercises; if you are not prepared for them, you will do well to abandon history for something less arduous.

As for imagination, that is in all likelihood something that cannot be cultivated; either you have it or you do not. If you do not have it you may be a worthy compiler of facts, a good analyst, a safe guide through the labyrinths of the past, but you will never be able to recreate that past, never set the blood coursing through the veins of your readers, or ideas tumbling over each other in their heads. As for "common sense"—alas it is by no means as common as the phrase implies. It is an all-inclusive term which embraces such disparate qualities as moderation, balance, judiciousness, critical intelligence, open-mindedness, tolerance, proportion, and good humor, and doubtless other qualities as well. Without it the most scholarly and interesting works misfire—for example as with William Crosskey's two learned volumes designed to prove that the Founding Fathers meant something quite different from what they said and wrote, or Otto Eisenschiml's elaborate proof that Secretary Stanton master-minded the plot to assassinate Lincoln, or Charles Tansill's well documented volumes designed to prove that Franklin Roosevelt instigated the Second World War, or—to take a more extreme example—those many volumes dedicated to the proposition that Lord Bacon or the Earl of Oxford, or somebody else wrote the plays hitherto attributed to Shakespeare.

Let us turn, then, to some practical considerations in the writing of history: first, the choice of a subject. That seems almost too elementary a matter to justify comment, but alas it is not. Again and again otherwise sensible neophyte historians come a cropper when they select a subject for their investigation. Here is where common sense comes in. Your subject should not be too ambitious, or too petty. It should not be too hackneyed, or too esoteric. It should be something you can manage within the time you have available, the time and the space. It should be something which has not been chewed up by generations of historians; at the same time it should not be something so strange and rare that it will be of interest only to you. Take care, too, that the materials you will need to use are not only available but available to you. Do not select some subject for which the materials are scanty and unreliable, or the essential documents inaccessible—some chapter in the history of the Secret Service, for example, or the CIA—or in the possession of a family which preserves them for its own purposes, or in the archives of Spain or Australia—unless indeed you happen to be bound for Spain or Australia. If you live in Montana do not select a subject which has to be studied in the files of eastern newspapers; if you live in New York City do not select a subject which has to be studied through materials scattered throughout a dozen western historical societies. If your command of languages is shaky, avoid subjects which require a knowledge of half a dozen foreign languages; if your eyesight is poor avoid subjects which are to be studied in seventeenth or eighteenth century manuscripts or—for that matter—in the manuscripts of Horace Greeley or Charles Sumner or others whose handwriting was notoriously indecipherable.

All of this is purely negative—this elimination of subjects that do not lend themselves to orderly treatment. There is one affirmative consideration equally basic and imperative: select a subject the way you would select a friend or, perhaps, a spouse. It is something you are going to live with for a long time, perhaps for years; select therefore a good companion for the journey. Ideally you should find a subject which so interests and excites you that you cannot resist it. On the whole it is desirable to choose a subject which enlists your sympathy, though that is by no means essential. You can write effectively about the Massacre of St. Bartholomew even though you disapprove in principle of religious intolerance; you can write perspicaciously of Hitler without approving of Nazism; yet it is perhaps best to avoid the first if you are of Huguenot descent and the second if you are Jewish.

For biographical subjects it is particularly important to find a figure who enlists your sympathy as well as your interest. As you would not want to live intimately with someone you heartily disliked, so you will not want to live on terms of intimacy with some historical character whom you heartily dislike. There are examples of biographers who have disliked—or come to dislike—their subject: Froude certainly appeared to dislike Carlyle—though in fact he did not—and Lytton Strachey had no use for his Eminent Victorians, while Paxton Hibben scarcely tried to conceal his contempt for William Jennings Bryan. But these are exceptions. The best biographers confess admiration and sympathy for their subjects, and some of them deep personal affection—Boswell's famous biography of Dr. Johnson, for example, or William Dean Howells' tender interpretation, *My Mark Twain,* or George Otto Trevelyan's spirited biography of his uncle, *Lord Macaulay.*

Once you have found a sympathetic subject, and ascertained that there is something new to be said about it and that the materials on which to base your study are ample and readily available, you can get started. And from now on common sense really does take charge.

Even here there are some practical observations that are relevant. The first is this: do not waste time and energy in what is amiably called "reading around" a subject. Reading around, or reading for background, is more often than not an excuse for not getting on with the job: it is pleasant, it is edifying—and it is inexhaustible. A chemist concerned with a specific problem does not stop to "read around" chemistry; a lawyer dealing with a specific case does not "read around" the law. Plunge into the subject itself; get your problem by the throat and grapple with it. The closer you come to it, and the deeper your understanding of it, the more surely you will become familiar with all the surrounding landscape. Gradually everything will fall into place. That, after all, is the natural way: you come only gradually to know the background of a friend, and even children do not fill in the background of parents and grandparents until they themselves have children. In short, start with the particular, not with the general; read deeply in the history of the particular, and you will find that the general takes care of itself.

A second practical rule is to begin almost at once collecting the essential materials for your essay or monograph and organizing them into some coherent pattern. Granted you do not really know what is "essential," or just what the pattern is to be; the sooner you get started, the sooner you will find answers to these questions. Do not think you have to read everything, take notes on everything, track down every reference, look at every piece of manuscript before you begin to write. The sooner you begin the better, for only as you write will you discover the lacunae in your knowledge, and fill them.

There is a third practical consideration here that has to do with the compilation of your materials. For most purposes that means "taking notes"—that arduous and never-ending process which can, unless you are careful, become something of an opiate, a pleasant substitute for the real work of thinking and writing. Not long ago taking notes meant precisely that; the scholar painfully, and painstakingly, copied out mountains of passages which he hoped would one day prove useful, or hired someone to do it for him. Now all of that has changed; note-taking has been mechanized, like so many other things, and the happy researcher now sends his materials off to be Photostated, Xeroxed or microfilmed—all much better than in the bad old days. Now you can get ten times as much copied, nay a hundred times as much; now you can be sure of accuracy; now you can save time and go everywhere and see everything! Fortunate scholars; now we may expect them all to write twice as much as any former generation. How odd that they write only half as much!

We are all immensely indebted to modern techniques of mechanical reproduction, but do not be carried away by them to the point where you think that history itself has become mechanized. It is all very well to have machines do your copying for you, but remember that they cannot think for you. Something is to be said for doing things yourself—even for copying documents yourself. The great literary historian Van Wyck Brooks, author of the most interesting of literary histories of America, did all his own copying and, what is more, did it all by hand. He could, of course, have employed copyists, or bought himself a copying machine. He preferred to do his own work because he knew what every scholar comes to know: that if you copy things yourself, you remember them. He knew, too, another important lesson: that the by-product of copying is often more important than the product, namely the ideas you get as you go. No machine can get those ideas for you, and there is no substitute for the inspiration which comes from your own direct, fresh, and uncomplicated relation with your materials.

When it comes to writing history, keep in mind that there are almost as many ways of writing as there are historians. There is no formula; you will have to find your own formula. There is no pattern; you will have to work out your own pattern. But this is not to suggest that there are no models. There are models by the score. You will doubtless be influenced by them, just as a painter is influenced by Rembrandt or Goya, Whistler or Picasso. That does not mean that you can successfully adopt for your own the lordly style of a Gibbon, the rhetorical style of a Carlyle, the balanced cadences of a Macaulay, the strong masculine style of a Mahan, the brilliant style of a Parrington, the epigrammatic style of a Philip Guedalla, the allusive style of a Denis Brogan, the intimate style of a Paul Hazard. All of these are available, but in writing, as in other matters, the style reflects the man and your style must reflect you.

But style is not a single or a static thing; you will want to vary your style, to adapt it to the subject matter. You would not think of using the same pattern of organization, the same style of presentation, for all subjects, any more than you would clothe all men and women alike at all times. A style suitable, let us say, to a history of the Tariff of 1890 is not a good style for a history of the conquest of Peru or for a biography of Herman Melville. Each subject makes its own claim upon you; each one demands individual treatment. Practiced historians know this almost instinctively, and vary their styles, as do professional couturiers or photographers. Thomas Beer, for example—he was a novelist as well as an historian—used very different styles in his biography of *Stephen Crane* and his essay on *The Mauve Decade;* John Morley varied his style to suit the different requirements of *Voltaire* and of *Gladstone;* Henry Adams had one style for the *History* and a quite different one for the *Education,* more subtle, more allusive, though not more brilliant.

Some Problems of History

chapter four

LIMITATIONS ON THE HISTORIAN

"The historian," writes Veronica Wedgwood, "ought to be the humblest of men; he is faced a dozen times a day with the evidence of his own ignorance; he is perpetually confronted with his own humiliating inability to interpret his material correctly; he is, in a sense that no other writer is, in bondage to that material." In bondage! Most sophisticated historians would readily agree with this. They are ever conscious of the limitations and handicaps under which they work, and of the temptations and dangers to which they are exposed. But the public tends to overlook these limitations, and some historians are even innocent enough, or brash enough, to gloss over the difficulties inherent in their profession.

History is in fact far more complex and disorderly than the amateur suspects. To most laymen it is all simple and straightforward. What is it, he asks, that you want to know? Is it the writing of the Magna Carta, the consolidation of Germany under Bismarck, the triumph of Communism in China? Get your facts, put them together in some sensible order, and Presto! there is your history. The great historian Henry Adams has made the classic observation on this notion of history. "He had even published a dozen volumes of American history," he recalled, "for no other purpose than to satisfy himself whether, by the severest process of stating, with the least possible comment, such facts as seemed sure in such order as seemed rigorously consequent, he could fix for a familiar moment a necessary sequence of human movement." The result, he confessed, was failure. "Where he saw sequence other men saw something quite different, and no one saw the same unit of measure," and he concluded that "the sequence of men led to nothing and that the sequence of their society could lead no further, while the mere sequence of time was artificial, and the sequence of thought was chaos." (*The Education of Henry Adams*, Boston: Houghton Mifflin Company, 1918, p. 382.) So he abandoned history altogether and asserted, somewhat perversely, that any nine pages of his novel, *Esther*, were worth more than the nine volumes of his *History*. Posterity does not agree with this verdict, but that is another matter.

What, then, are some of these limitations which have discouraged so many historians, and which, Miss Wedgwood admonished us, should induce humility?

First, there are the many and sobering limitations on historical materials. There is, for example, the role of fortuity. The chemist or biologist can command whatever materials he needs for his experiments, but the historian works with what happens to come to hand. What we are permitted "to know" is not only but a small part of "what happened in history," but it is a miscellany which has come to us in large part by chance rather than by choice. What we can see of history is far less than what we can see of the iceberg; most of it, too, is buried and forever lost. It is lost because it was never compiled; it is lost because of the erosion of time—fire and water and weather and carelessness; it is lost because it was deliberately destroyed. How do we know that what has come down to us is either the most important or the most authentic representation of any chapter of past history?

Another limitation is that of distortion; the record of the past, as we have it, is monstrously lopsided. Thus we know a great deal of the history of some European peoples, and because this record is available we confuse it with History and write as if it embraced the whole of the past. It is not merely that the records for most non-European societies are non-existent or lost—the African, for example, or the American Indian or the Carthagenian—but that even where records are available—in China, or in India for example—western historians have not used them. This is easy to understand, but we should not call what we choose to interest ourselves in History, and formulate broad, even universal, generalizations on the basis of such fragmentary and arbitrary evidence.

The very fact that history is based so largely on the written record introduces a note of unbalance, and distorts our view. For what it inevitably means is that we exaggerate the role of the written record and of those peoples who did keep records at the expense of those who did not, or whose records are fitful and uninformative. Almost every historian has an unconscious bias in favor of the literary history-conscious, western European, and against the others: in favor of the Jews and against the Babylonians, in favor of the Greeks and against the Persians, in favor of the Romans and against the "barbarians." Even in highly sophisticated societies such as our own we must acknowledge a distortion induced by the charms of the written record. How much of American history has been colored by the fact that New Englanders have been more assiduous in keeping records and more effective in presenting them than, let us say, Virginians or Carolinians; Jamestown came before Plymouth, but every schoolboy knows, from poetry, fiction, and painting as well as from history, the story of the Pilgrims and the Puritans. The slave-owner was literate and articulate, the Negro slave illiterate and inarticulate; it was, until recently, the slave-owner's version of slavery which came down to us and which was widely accepted as history.

The seduction, or tyranny, of the written record introduces another element of distortion, namely, that what attracts the record-keeper and the historian is the dramatic, the spectacular, the bizarre, and the catastrophic. This has always been true, and it remains true today, as reference to any daily newspaper will make clear. The monkish chroniclers who bequeathed us so many records did not customarily record the daily routine of life, but only events which they considered out of the ordinary or miraculous: comets and earthquakes and plagues and wars; and millions of families have endorsed this view of history by recording in their family Bibles only births, marriages, and deaths. The historian too is attracted by whatever is dramatic or unusual or romantic; he writes the annals of the rich and the great; for the annals of the poor, as we know, are short and simple. How natural it is for us, how inevitable perhaps, to believe that history is, by its very nature, the record of what is dramatic and astonishing. A great statesman, a soldier, an explorer, we say "makes history"; or a particular people at a particular time—the Athenians of the fifth century B.C., or the French during their Revolution, "make history." This is, of course, nonsense; everybody makes history all the time, the Slave as well as the Master, the South Sea Islander as well as the Parisian. What we mean is that these people make the kind of history that appeals to us, that we happen to know about, and that we like to write about; it follows very easily that what appeals to us and what we write about is history.

Closely associated with the enchantment of the dramatic is the spell of the familiar. So accustomed are we to the formal patterns of history that it requires a convulsive effort for us to remember that these are not history's patterns, but ours. We have already considered the dangers latent in familiar chronological and regional patterns—the habit of dividing history into neat packets labelled Ancient, Medieval, and

Modern, or of carving up American history into Colonial, Revolutionary, Middle Period, and so forth. There is a further refinement on these divisions which is even more artificial, the habit of forcing history into the straitjackets of monarchical or presidential patterns. Thus we write of the Age of Louis XIV or of Napoleon, of the Jeffersonian era, or the era of Franklin D. Roosevelt.

Of all patterns which we have imposed upon history, it is the national which is the most powerful and the most pervasive, and perhaps the most mischievous. The limitations which nationalism imposes upon history go far beyond those of providing convenient but misleading patterns; we shall deal at greater length with these further limitations.

The parochialism of nationalism or of race is familiar, and most of us try to guard against it. We are less aware of and more vulnerable to another form of parochialism, the parochialism of time. Present-mindedness is, perhaps, the most intractable of all the limitations on history—our instinctive habit of looking at the past through our own eyes, judging it by our own standards, recreating it in our own words or reading back into the language of the past our own meanings, assuming that whatever happened, happened in some "past" and forgetting that every past was once a present. As that wise counsellor, Frederic Maitland, reminds us:

> If we speak, we must speak with words; if we think we must think with thoughts. We are moderns, and our words and thoughts cannot but be modern. Perhaps . . . it is too late for us to be early English. Every thought will be too sharp, every word will imply too many contrasts. We must, it is to be feared, use many words and qualify our every statement until we have almost contradicted it. ("Township and Borough.")

It is probable that we are, to a large degree, helpless in this matter; try as we will we cannot "think ourselves back into a twilight," to use Maitland's wonderful phrase. We cannot really put ourselves inside the minds, or skins, of Cyrus, or Brutus, or Joan of Arc, or the Indian chief Pontiac. That we do try is a tribute to the rigor of our historical conscience, and a few great histories and biographies are monuments to the fact that we are not always unsuccessful, though in the nature of the case we are not permitted to know even this. But the difficulty of present-mindedness is really deeper. It is that we almost instinctively assume that the past was made just for us, that it is interesting only insofar as it caters to our current interests, and significant only when it has ostentatious consequences for us. How easily we fall into what might be called the fallacy of "quaintness"—the fallacy of supposing that Medieval People were medieval in their own eyes as well, or that Renaissance Man betrays us if he does not live up to our notion of what he should be, or that the Forefathers knew that they were Forefathers. How hard it is for us to realize that the past was as real to those who lived in it as the present is to us and that they no more lived for our edification than we live for the edification of distant future generations.

There is another danger implicit in present-mindedness, one, again, which we cannot, in the nature of things, escape, but against which we must everlastingly guard ourselves. That is what we may call the danger of the *fait accompli*. We know what happened in history and because we know it, we can never look back upon it with the eyes of innocence. We know that the Athenian expedition to Syracuse is going to fail; that Rome will humble Carthage, and the Roman Republic change into an empire; that the Moslems will eventually be driven out of western Europe, and that Christianity will triumph; that it is the English who will win the struggle for the American continent; that no matter how dark the outlook Washington will lead his ragged army to victory at Yorktown; that no matter how glittering the prospects, Robert E. Lee is headed for Appomattox. We are, all of us, in the position of the reader of mystery stories who reads the last chapter first. But we should remember that we do not know how our own history is going to come out, and neither did earlier generations of men.

Our inability to divorce ourselves from knowing how history is going to come out almost guarantees that our view of the past will be astigmatic. We inevitably read back into the past what we know occurred, and adopt a *post hoc propter hoc* attitude toward history. As Rome is bound to fall to the barbarian invaders we find explanations of that fall in the corruption and immorality of public life; as Britain is doomed to lose her American colonies, we accept Tom Paine's observation that it is absurd for a continent to belong to an island; as the Confederacy is predestined to defeat we confidently find the causes of that defeat. But if we adopt these positions, we render ourselves incapable of understanding the past in its own terms. As David Donald has said, historians are camp-followers of victorious armies. Knowing which side is going to win—the Romans, Christianity, the Union, the Atlantic powers—they instinctively ally themselves with the winning side; they look for explanations of what triumphed and ignore the evidence on the other side. Some of them see the hand of God, or of Progress, or of Evolution, in whatever triumphed and whatever failed.

Nothing, surely, is more fatal to the integrity of historical investigation than the doctrine of inevitability implicit in this attitude. For if whatever happened in history was inevitable, whether because it expressed the will of God or the force of evolution or of progress, then there is little point in conducting any investigation whatsoever into the causes or the consequences of things. *Felix qui potuit rerum cognoscere causas,* but if the causes of things are predestined, there is no happiness, and no value either. As Charles A. Beard warned us:

> If all human affairs were reduced to law, to a kind of terrestial mechanics, a chief end of the quest, that is, human control over human occurrences and actions, would itself become meaningless. Should'mankind discover the law of its total historical unfolding, then it would be imprisoned in its own fate, and powerless to change it; the past, present and future would be revealed as fixed and beyond the reach of human choice and will. Men and women would be chained to their destinies as the stars and tides are to their routine. (*The Open Door at Home,* New York: The Macmillan Company, p. 14.)

But, as far as we know, the course of history is not predestined. Life has always been, as it is now, "a roar of bargain and of battle," and the intellectual challenge to understand the past is no less compelling than the challenge to understand the present and the future. There is, to be sure, one sobering difference here. If we understand the present we may be able to command it, but there is no way by which we can command the past.

THE TROUBLE WITH FACTS

These are some of the limitations on the historian. But there are limitations inherent in the facts of history, as well.

Poor, despised facts, they have a hard time. Nobody believes in them; nobody has any faith in them. With almost a single voice historians say that there are no facts, none that can be relied upon anyway; there are only some agreed-on assumptions which we choose to call facts so we can get on with the job. But do not be misled by them, do not take them seriously, or they will betray you. Facts are subjective, they exist in the mind of the historian, they change their character with each historian. The facts of the Franco-Prussian War are one thing to a French historian, another to a German; the facts about the creation of the state of Israel read very differently in the eyes of Jews and Arabs. Facts are like the Cheshire cat, in *Alice in Wonderland;* as we look at them they fade away, all but the grin.

What is the trouble with facts?

First, a paradox. There are too few facts, and there are too many. There are far too few facts about immense areas of past history. How little we know, after all, about most of mankind—about the people of Asia, of Africa, of pre-Columbian America; how little we know about lost people like the Carthaginians and the Etruscans, the early Celts and the Basques. How little we know about the remote past, as contrasted with the recent past. How do we dare reconstruct the ancient world with any assurance, when our knowledge is confined to small areas around the Mediterranean; yet we confidently call this Ancient History. How can we write with any assurance about the history of the American continents when—except for what ethnology and archeology may tell us—our knowledge embraces only five centuries out of a possible twenty-five thousand years? How little we know—even in modern times—of the lives of the poor, of those vast majorities of each generation about whom we have no reliable facts.

And, at the other end of the spectrum, we know almost too much about the modern history of the west—America, Britain, France, Germany, Italy in the nineteenth or twentieth centuries. We are overwhelmed by mountains of evidence; it accumulates faster than even computers can record it, and we still have to process the material from the computers. We do not and cannot have all the facts about the Second World War, but it is safe to conjecture that historians will never get through the miles of filing cases of historical records now resting in warehouses throughout the country. Inevitably our vision of the past is distorted by this disproportion in our evidence; inevitably we translate this disproportion into historical distortions.

We have already noted the role of caprice and fortuity in the historical record, and the influence of modern-mindedness and of subjectivity. There are still further limitations on "facts." There is for example the elementary consideration that we can rarely attain factual accuracy about the past, even about the recent past. The uninitiated take factual accuracy for granted in history as they take it for granted in chemistry or physics, but as soon as they try to reconstruct any chapter of past history they speedily discover that accuracy is unattainable. The science of statistics is new, and even such statistics as we have are rarely reliable. We do not know such fundamental things as the populations or the birth and death rates of ancient peoples; we do not know the numbers in armies or in battles, or the casualties in war. We do not know the value or the volume of farm production or of domestic industries or of trade. Even in modern history, statistics often fail us: we do not and probably cannot know with any accuracy the number of soldiers in the Union or the Confederate armies, or the losses, or the cost of the war; the ascertainable "facts" do not go very far in explaining why Britain did not intervene on the side of the Confederacy. Even so apparently elementary a matter as the total acreage of public lands granted by state and federal governments to American railroads has long been and still is a matter of conjecture and debate.

On these, and a hundred other important questions of history, we can only make educated guesses.

There are, to be sure, some matters about which we can be accurate and certain, but alas, these turn out to be matters of no great importance. We can be accurate about the succession of American Presidents, or of the kings of England or France, and we prefer an historian who knows that Buchanan succeeded Pierce, and not the other way around, and who can list the Richards and the Henrys, the Philips and the Louis in their proper order. This is too elementary to be helpful. We can be accurate about the dates of the Buchanan administration, but not about Buchanan's role in the coming of the Civil War; we can be accurate about the dates for Louis XVI, but there is no agreement on his contribution to the breakdown of the *ancien régime*.

Finally, the facts of history turn out to be not hard and objective but impalpable and subjective. Ranke and his successors taught us to rely on documents for our history; the documents, they were confident, would speak for themselves. Alas, they do not speak for themselves. They speak, rather, for us, and with a hundred different voices, usually raucous and clashing. They tell us not what actually happened but, more often than not, what we want to hear. Take, for example, the two most famous documents of American history—the Declaration of Independence and the federal Constitution. Even the textual history of the Declaration is an intricate affair, but look aside from the textual history to the political and philosophical. Here are the immortal words—their immortality, note, not inherent, but conferred upon them by later generations—what do they mean? What did Jefferson and the members of the Continental Congress mean when he wrote, and they endorsed, the statement that "all men are created equal"? What did he mean when he wrote, what did they mean when they endorsed, the sentiment that the "pursuit of happiness" is an unalienable right?

No two people read quite the same thing into these words. Certainly the generation of Thomas Jefferson (even the term "generation" is an artificial one, and if we accept Jefferson's own calculation of a generation as twenty years, he belonged to four!) and our own generation read different meanings into terms like "equality" and "happiness." Certainly, too, in our own day, men and women read different meanings into the word "happiness," and northerners and southerners, whites and Negroes, read different meanings into the term "equality." It requires a lifetime of study to understand these esoteric words, and after a lifetime of study different historians come up with very different explanations. Clearly this famous document does not speak for itself.

Contemplate, then, the Constitution of the United States, a document of some six thousand carefully chosen words, simple, lucid, logical. Does the Constitution speak for itself? Clearly it does not; if it did we should not need the 375 volumes of Supreme Court *Reports* to explain and interpret it, nor would learned and upright judges on the Supreme Court so frequently disagree about the meaning of such phrases as "commerce among the several states," "the executive power," "impair the obligation of contracts," "common defense and general welfare," "necessary and proper," and "due process of law."

Or take another kind of document: a painting. Does the meaning of the painting inhere in the painting itself? Not entirely. You can look at it and see a great deal which you have missed; an art historian or art critic can look at it through the eyes of history and see many things which escape the rest of us and some, perhaps, which were not in the mind of the artist when he painted the picture.

Take for example, the various paintings by Poussin on the theme *Et in Arcadia Ego,* which Edwin Panofsky has dealt with in a fascinating essay on that subject. To the onlooker it is a simple matter—shepherds and maidens stumbling on a tomb with that touching inscription are struck into sober contemplation by the realization that others before them had lived in Arcadia and now were dead and gone. But is that really what the paintings mean, or what the phrase and the concept originally meant? Not at all, says Panofsky. What they mean is not "I too have lived in Arcadia," but "Death, too, is in Arcadia." That reverses the moral of the pictures completely; it is no longer a reminder that every generation has known happiness, but a reminder that death is ever present, even in Arcadia. But hold, it is not that simple, either, for eighteenth century painters did in fact reverse the original meaning. Unwilling to contemplate the presence of death in Arcadia, they turned the whole thing into a pastoral scene, one designed to show that generation was linked to generation by happiness, not by death.

Contemplate another, and more familiar, artistic document: Emanuel Leutze's painting of "Washington Crossing the Delaware." Clearly this is not a contemporary record: there were no artists present to record that famous crossing. It was painted three-quarters of a century after the event; the river was the Rhine, not the Delaware, and Washington was Worthington Whittredge, a young American artist studying in Düsseldorf. The scene itself was a product of Leutze's romantic imagination. If Washington had stood up in that rowboat he would have fallen overboard; the flag was quite incorrect; and as the crossing was made before dawn of a winter night, neither Washington nor the sailors who rowed him would have been visible in the dark. But all that was of no importance. The painting had a life of its own. It was accepted with rapture as an authentic representation; it made its way at once into the minds and hearts of the American people; it has come to be, for all practical purposes, the authentic representation of the historic event. If it does not reproduce an historical fact it is, itself, an historical fact.

A document, then, may mean many things. Its meaning is to be understood in the light of its own contemporary history; it is to be understood in the light of the reason, temperament, and prejudices of the historian who uses it; it is to be arrived at and interpreted through the symbolism it communicates. Even that is not the end of it. For the historian has to communicate with each individual reader, and each one will read the document or the analysis in his own way, just as each individual looks at a Whistler painting or listens to a Mozart sonata in his own way.

The facts of history are fragmentary, elusive, and subjective. But that is true of most of these studies which engage the minds and the passions of men—art and letters, morals and ethics, even law and politics, as every judge and statesman knows. We must not expect things to be easier for the historian than they are for those many others who try somehow to reconcile the heritage of the past—its laws and principles and monuments—with the imaginations, the passions, the emotions, and the facts of their own time. It is not of history, but of the whole cargo of thought and character and habit that William Vaughn Moody wrote those moving lines:

> This earth is not the steadfast thing
> We landsmen build upon;
> From deep to deep she varies pace,
> And while she comes is gone.
> Beneath my feet I feel,
> Her smooth bulk heave and dip;
> With velvet plunge and soft upreel
> She swings and steadies to her keel
> Like a gallant, gallant ship.
>
> ("Gloucester Moors")

Yet though we admit the limitations and difficulties of history, item by item, if we take them too hard, we will find ourselves out of a job. If the limitations really are so severe, and the facts really are so elusive, we may be forced to give up history altogether. If we are to get on with the job, we must agree upon some kind of factual foundation or framework for our histories, if only that Washington was in fact the first President of the United States, or that the United States did in fact fight a war with Mexico which brought her Texas and California, or that Lincoln was in fact assassinated. For, treacherous as they no doubt are, facts are like syntax and grammar; we need them as a framework and a mechanism if we are to make ourselves clear. There is nothing sacred about grammar, and a wide latitude is permitted in its usage, but if we are perpetually to stop and question the authority of our grammar we will never finish what we are saying or writing.

Historians have, after all, surmounted the difficulties that crowd about them, and given us famous and affluent histories. Gibbon was aware of the difficulties, and Macaulay, Ranke and Mommsen, Maitland and Holdsworth, Parkman and Henry Adams, yet all of them managed to write histories which have enlarged the thoughts and lifted the spirits of generations of men. Let the young historian take to heart the lines of the Greek Anthology:

> A shipwrecked sailor, buried on this coast
> Bids you set sail;
> Full many a gallant bark, when we were lost
> Weathered the gale.

INTERPRETATION—AND BIAS

Let us admit at once that history is neither scientific nor mechanical, that the historian is human and therefore fallible, and that the ideal history, completely objective and dispassionate, is an illusion. There is bias in the choice of a subject, bias in the selection of material, bias in its organization and presentation, and, inevitably, bias in its interpretation. Consciously, or unconsciously, all historians are biased: they are creatures of their time, their race, their faith, their class, their country—creatures, and even prisoners.

Most historians strive manfully to avoid bias and achieve objectivity when they teach or write history, but there have always been some who out of defiance, or out of acquiescence to the inevitable, have accepted the fact of bias and tried to make a virtue of it. The famous German historian, Heinrich von Treitschke, represents the first attitude. Writing in 1865 he asserted that a "bloodless objectivity which does not say on which side is the narrator's heart, is the exact opposite of the true historical sense," and in his own many-volumed *History of Germany in the Nineteenth Century* he left no one in doubt about what side his heart was on, or his mind and his temper either. The American Charles A. Beard represents the second attitude. "Any selection and arrangement of facts," he said in his address on "History as an Act of Faith," "pertaining to any large area of History, either local or world, race or class, is controlled inexorably by the frame of reference in the mind of the selector or arranger." As long as this was true, he concluded, it was only honorable for the historian frankly to acknowledge his "frame of reference"—that is, his bias. And, as history is, inevitably, an instrument of propaganda, said Beard, let us take care that it is propaganda for good causes, for peace and progress, for justice and truth, and not for bad.

Pity the poor historian. He is the victim, the prisoner, of circumstances, of Nature and of human nature. Even St. Anthony was not exposed to so many temptations. Is he a modern man: then how will he ever understand medieval man? Is he a European: can he ever really understand and do justice to the world of Asia and of Africa—or even of America? Is he a white man: can he really understand the colored peoples who constitute three-quarters of the human race? Is he a Christian: can he do justice to those he has learned to designate pagans or heathens? Is he a Catholic: can he be fair to Protestants? Is he a Protestant: can he be fair to the Papacy and the Inquisition? Is he—and he almost certainly is—a member of the middle or the upper classes, literate and educated: can he really understand the point of view of the workingman and the peasant? Can a liberal like Macaulay do justice to the Stuarts? Can a Marxist like Albert Mathiez do justice to the *ancien régime*—or even to the Gironde? Can a Republican like Albert Beveridge understand Jefferson or a Democrat like Claude Bowers understand Hamilton or a New Dealer like Arthur Schlesinger, Jr., be fair to Herbert Hoover? Can a Georgia gentleman like Ulrich B. Phillips ever really understand slavery? Can a Negro Marxist like W. E. B. Du Bois write dispassionately of slaveholders or of southern Bourbons? Can an Englishman or an Irishman, a German or a Frenchman be expected to emancipate himself from his national predilections, and write history that gives no hint of national affiliations or loyalties?

It was the hope of Lord Acton that a new generation of historians could answer all these questions in the affirmative. When, in 1896, he launched the co-operative *Cambridge Modern History,* he told potential contributors that "we shall avoid the needless utterance of opinion or service of a cause. Contributors will understand that our Waterloo must satisfy French and English, Germans and Dutch alike; that nobody can tell, without examining the list of authors, where the Bishop of Oxford laid down the pen and whether Fairbairn or Gasquet, Liebermann or Harrison, took it up." But few historians have ever really managed to live up to these austere standards, and it is doubtful whether Acton did himself.

It is easy enough to discern bias in history, easy enough to recognize a great deal of what passes for history as propaganda of varying degrees of subtlety. Much of this propaganda does not rise to the dignity of history—the histories, put out by Nazi historians, designed to prove the superiority of the Aryan race and the virtue of Hitlerian Germany; the "new-think" put out by Communist historians to justify every turn and twist of Communist policy. But we should remember, too, that some of the most influential works of history have been propaganda: Clarendon's classic *History of the Rebellion,* for example, or the Abbé Raynal's *Philosophical History of the Indies*—an "instrument of war" against the Church—or Frederic Masson's adulatory but learned biography of Napoleon, or Henry Wilson's *Rise and Fall of the Slave Power in America.* In our own day we can readily discern elements of propaganda, or partisanship, in such major works as Charles A. Beard's studies of American foreign policy between the wars, or Parrington's brilliant *Main Currents of American Thought,* or Winston Churchill's *World Crisis,* but we do not really think the worse of them for that.

Actually partisanship often adds zest to historical writing; for partisanship is an expression of interest and excitement and passion, and these can stir the reader as judiciousness might not. Certainly Macaulay lives, while Stubbs and Gardiner are read only by the specialists; Motley's thrilling story of the *Rise of the Dutch Republic* has inspired generations of readers with enthusiasm for liberty and detestation of tyranny which cannot be wholly misguided; Parrington, for all his faults, excites an interest in American literature that no other historian or critic has been able to equal; Winston Churchill's splendid tributes to English courage had consequences to history that no other histories of this century could match. As that immaculate historian Lord Acton himself observed, "the strongest and most impressive personalities . . . project their own broad shadows upon their pages. This is a practice proper to great men, and a great man may be worth several immaculate historians."

Let us, then, not be too distressed that history is unscientific, partisan and hopelessly subjective; that it lends itself so readily to misrepresentation and even to propaganda; that it reflects, for better or for worse, the personality, the prejudices, the idiosyncrasies of historians. The subjectivity is inevitable; the partisanship is regrettable, but has compensations; the propaganda usually takes care of itself, for it carries with it a kind of built-in discount; the idiosyncrasy is almost always interesting. And let us remember, too, that nothing which deals with human beings can approach scientific objectivity, that there is no wholly impartial justice, no wholly impartial political, economic, or social theory, no impartial education.

There is one bias, one prejudice, one obsession, so pervasive and so powerful that it deserves special consideration: nationalism. History, which should be the most cosmopolitan of studies, most catholic in its sympathies, most ecumenical in its interests, has, in the past century and a half, become an instrument of nationalism.

Nationalism is, no doubt, the most powerful force in modern history, and it is scarcely surprising that it should have captured historiography and enslaved historians. The historian no longer writes in a universal language—Latin for example, or, in the eighteenth century, French—but in the national vernacular; he adapts his history to a national framework, depends on national archives and similar sources for materials, and almost inevitably expresses a national point of view. In the eighteenth century the ardors of nationalism were moderated by rationalism and cosmopolitanism, and if such books as Hume's *England*, Robertson's *Scotland* or Müller's *Switzerland* threw history a bit out of focus, they did no serious violence to historical truth. Very different was the nationalist history which came in, as on flood tide, with the French Revolution and Napoleon, and with modern, chauvinistic, nationalism. The new history reflected national interests, prejudices, and passions or, worse, stimulated them. It is a far cry from the cool rationalism of Robertson's *Scotland* to the romantic lyricism of Michelet's *France*, the savage chauvinism of Treitschke's *Germany*, the patriotic passion of Francis Palacky's *History of the Bohemian People*, or even the ardent enthusiasm of George Bancroft's *History of the United States*.

Nationalism, as we know it, is both recent and parochial. It was invented by western Europeans—British, French, Germans—and has flourished for less than 200 years. For historians to confuse it with universal history or—as some do—with the cosmic system, to read into it absolute values and absolute virtues, to identify themselves—and truth—passionately with one nation rather than another, is to betray history itself. It is to violate what should be the historical categorical imperative: never to subordinate the whole to the part, the permanent to the transient, the end to the means.

Overt bias, such as that which responds to nationalism, is easy to detect and not difficult to discount. There is a more subtle form of bias which is implicit in and all but inextricable from that present-mindedness which we considered earlier. This is sometimes called the problem of *nunc pro tunc*: the now for the then, the present for the past. What point of view should the historian adopt when he deals with the past, or with societies and civilizations very different from his own? Should he maintain his own standards and values, or should he try to adopt the standards and values of the peoples and the age with which he is concerned?

At first glance this problem seems easy enough: the right and proper thing to do is to adopt the measure and the standards of the era and the people we are trying to understand and to explain. How absurd, after all, to judge the Persians, or even the Egyptians or the Greeks, by the standards of modern England; how absurd to judge the American Indian by the standards of eighteenth century Europe; how misguided to apply our own artistic standards to ancient China or India, our intellectual and scientific standards to the Middle Ages. No, let us rather enter into the minds and the spirits of the people we are studying. So said Ranke, and all those who, after him, developed what it is fashionable to call Historicism. Let us so immerse ourselves in the past that we can see with their eyes, hear with their ears, think as they thought, and feel as they must have felt: only by emancipating ourselves from the present and re-entering into the past can we be true to history; only by this renunciation of our own personalities can we hope to recover the character of the past.

This ideal was hopefully advanced in a recent biography of the "Great American Preacher" Theodore Parker:

> I have tried to know and to feel what Parker and his friends knew and felt, to accept the limitations of their minds, and, perhaps, of their characters. I have tried to see men and measures with Parker's eyes, to react to the events of the time as he did, or as I think that he did. I have permitted Parker to act as he chose to act, to render such judgment as he wished to make, to love those friends whom he did love, and to disparage those persons whom he disliked, whether he was wise in all this, or unwise. Where he was vain I have not sought to rebuke his vanity, where he was inconsistent I have not thought it necessary to remark his inconsistency, where he was ungenerous I have not taken him to task, where he was violent I have not tried to abate his violence, where he was mistaken I have not attempted to set him right; all of these things he confessed in his own words and actions and they appear without my intervention. (H. S. Commager, *Theodore Parker*, Boston: Little, Brown and Company, 1936, preface.)

Douglas Freeman, the distinguished biographer of Robert E. Lee, attempted to achieve this goal by the somewhat mechanical method of limiting himself, quite rigorously, to knowing only what Lee knew, and writing entirely within that framework of knowledge or of ignorance. Still another method of recreating the past is that used by two masters of intellectual history, the American, Van Wyck Brooks, and the Frenchman, Paul Hazard; it is the technique of literary intimacy. Here is M. Hazard describing the adventurers of the eighteenth century:

> In those days no one would stop in one place. Here was Montesquieu, off on the search for political constitutions; Diderot, after holding out against the idea for a long time, at length made the journey to Russia. Then, one fine day, the youthful Goldsmith resolves to set out for the Continent, and set out he does, without a penny to his name, with no one to fall back on in case of need, and with no definite itinerary in view. However, off he goes, playing his flute at cottage doors in the hope of getting, maybe, a bowl of soup or a shake-down in a barn. Holberg says

good-bye to Denmark, and takes to the road, relying on his fine voice, as Goldsmith on his flute-playing, to get him along. On he goes, from country to country, learns French in Paris, and teaches it at Oxford. He was not a man to be baulked by trifles. All these inquiring gentlemen, indeed, are as mobile as can be, and they are never satisfied, they've never seen enough. Exile brings them no repining. They don't mind knocking at strange doors, and the bread of the stranger leaves no bitterness in the mouth. Tossed by fate far beyond their native land, they profit by the occasion to improve their knowledge and shape their minds anew. Voltaire has no bad time of it in London. . . Nor does the Abbé Prévost fare so badly in Holland. Anyhow, that's where he sows his wild oats, and pretty plentifully, withal. . . . And Bolingbroke soon made himself at home as a noble lord of France, with his mansion and his ornamental gardens. He gathers a following about him, and wields the intellectual sceptre. Wincklemann finds his spiritual home in Italy. Look at the host of persecuted philosophers that crowded around Frederick in Berlin. No fugitives craving sanctuary, these; no more exiles; now we call them *cosmopolites.* (*European Thought in the Eighteenth Century,* London: Hollis and Carter, 1954, pp. 249–250.)

This is all admirable, but does it really enable us to recapture the past? We may believe that we can think as Theodore Parker thought, or know only what General Lee knew, or live and feel with the *philosophes,* but perhaps we delude ourselves.

For when we turn to the past and use the literature or the monuments of the past as a means of entering into its mind and spirit, how do we know that we have chosen correctly? The *philosophes* whom Hazard celebrates left an immense and entrancing literature, but did they really speak for France or for Germany in the eighteenth century? The Abolitionists of New England were incomparably articulate, but they were few in number and of feeble influence; they speak for themselves, to be sure, but do they speak for New England? We can, of course, confine ourselves to single individuals; we can spend a lifetime immersing ourselves in the writings of Jefferson or Edmund Burke or Napoleon until we come, at last, to think as these men thought. Ah, but do we? How does it happen that men who have in fact spent a lifetime with these great figures come up with such different reports?

We can doubtless do quite well in understanding the past—where the literature is voluminous, where the society is familiar, and where the past is recent. But what shall we say of the attempt to enter into the minds and thoughts of a distant or unfamiliar past—of the Spartans, for example, who differed so profoundly from the Athenians; of the Aztecs or the Incas whose records are fragmentary; of the Danes who invaded and harried England in the ninth century? Perhaps we can manage to understand Jefferson or Burke; can we manage to understand the Persian Cyrus, or Eric the Red?

There are many things to be said for accepting our limitations and looking at the past through the eyes of the present, but this is the most persuasive: no matter how hard we try, that is what we do anyway. We see the past through our own eyes, translate its language into our own, find interesting the things that interest us, and find significant the events that have had consequences for us. All this helps explain why each generation rewrites the history of the past: the view depends upon the point of view.

Consider, for example, the vicissitudes of the interpretation of Reconstruction by American historians.

Only half a century ago almost all students learned that after Appomattox the North imposed upon the stricken South a Punic peace, and they learned, too, that almost everything that happened—or failed to happen—thereafter could be blamed on the sins of Reconstruction. Through the tears that streamed from our sympathetic eyes we read that the federal government confiscated two billion dollars worth of slave property, that it imposed military rule upon the helpless South, that it forced—or tried to force—Negro equality upon a proud people long before the Negro was ready for equality or for anything; that it tolerated maladministration and corruption such as had never been known before in American history. In fact that generation of historians— the generation that ruled the roost during the first third of the twentieth century—was so ashamed of what the nation had done to the South that it almost apologized for fighting and winning the Civil War. Lee was the hero, not Grant, Confederate gray the stylish uniform, not Union blue, and everyone sang "Dixie Land." But now we look back on Reconstruction through very different eyes—or very different historical glasses. Now we regard it from the point of view of a generation that has lived through a war incomparably more savage and more destructive than the Civil War, and through peace-making incomparably more implacable than any that came in 1865. We have lost some of that innocence which still survived through the Victorian Age and into the new century, and lost our capacity to be surprised at ruthlessness, harshness, vindictiveness. Now when we look back at the American Civil War and Reconstruction it is with eyes that have seen what happened to the White Russians when the Bolsheviks won out; what happened to the Spanish Loyalists when Franco won out; what happened to the rebels first against Batista and then against Castro in Cuba; what happened to those desperate officers who tried to overthrow Hitler in 1944. And when we look at Reconstruction not from a provincial

American but from a world point of view we see that in all modern history no civil war was concluded with so little blood-letting or vindictiveness, and that in all modern history there is no example of magnanimity to compare with that which Lincoln and the national government displayed towards the defeated rebels. Now instead of writing the history of Reconstruction in terms of a Punic peace, we say rather that it was a magnanimous peace; instead of emphasizing the loss to slave-holders we emphasize the victory for Negro slaves; instead of deploring the establishment of military rule in the South we are astonished that the civil authority was so speedily restored and that the South was back in the Union—and even running it—within a few years. Instead of lamenting the fate of Jefferson Davis, languishing in prison for over a year, we note that after the greatest civil war of the century not one rebel lost his life, not one was proscribed, except briefly. And now, too, we re-examine—once again—the role of President Andrew Johnson, who first excited our reprobation and then our sympathies, and of the Radicals, who for a time excited our admiration, and then our contempt. We re-examine these in the light of recent developments in the position of the Negro in American life, and ask whether the Radical program might not have set the Negro question on the way to solution instead of leaving it for us to grapple with a century later. It would be presumptuous to say which of these points of view was the right one, for it is clear that there is no "right" point of view. What is clear is that, try how they will, historians see the past through the eyes of the present.

There is a final commentary on what is called Historicism. Even those who are most anxious to avoid imposing their own standards on the past and strive most sincerely to see the past in its own terms are tempted to make one exception to their principle. That is in the realm of moral judgment. Let us not force the past into the straitjacket of the present, they say, but at the same time let us not suspend the eternal rules of right and wrong.

And this brings us to the troublesome problem of moral judgment in history.

JUDGMENT IN HISTORY

To judge or not to judge, that is the historical question. Should the historian sit in judgment over the great drama of the past and the men and women who performed on that vast and crowded stage, exposing evil and celebrating virtue and damning and praising famous men? Or should he observe the historical processes with scientific detachment, and record them as automatically as a tape-recorder, rigorously excluding personal, national, or religious considerations? Is he competent to perform either of these functions—the function of the judge, or the function of the impartial reporter?

The problem is difficult and perhaps insoluble. It raises hard questions about the purpose of history, the duties and responsibilities of the scholar, the nature of historical judgment, and the distinctions, if any, between what might be called moral and secular judgment. It raises questions, too, about the competence of any historian to judge the past, and the sanctions, if any, behind such judgments as are rendered. And it requires us to weigh the dangers implicit in moral neutrality against those inherent in moral arrogance and intellectual parochialism.

Earlier generations of historians were not seriously troubled by this problem of judgment. The Greek historians, Herodotus and Thucydides, were surprisingly free from the urge to judge, but their successors in the ancient world took for granted that their function was to edify, to instruct, and to judge. Livy invited his readers to ponder the moral lessons taught by the history of Rome—as he presented it—and to observe how Rome rose to greatness through her virtues, and how the decay of these virtues brought ruin. Tacitus thought the highest function of history was to "rescue merit from oblivion," and "to hold out the reprobation of posterity as a warning and a rebuke to all base conduct." Plutarch, who wrote some sixty Moral Essays, compiled his famous *Parallel Lives* not to adorn a tale, but to point a moral, and succeeded beyond his farthest imagination.

Medieval historians knew perfectly well what were the moral standards to which history was obliged to conform, and knew, too, the penalties of non-conformity, for what was history but the working out of God's will with man? Even the great eighteenth century historians, Gibbon and Hume and Robertson, Rollin and Voltaire and Raynal, accepted Bolingbroke's aphorism that history was "philosophy teaching by examples," and they assumed that its lessons were moral and that it was the duty of the historian to point them. Only with the rise of "historicism" in the nineteenth century—there were antecedents, to be sure, in such historians as Machiavelli and Vico—did the question of the propriety and the validity of moral judgment come to the fore. Ranke, and his successors and disciples in almost every country, abjured moral judgment, or said that they did, and set themselves the task of simply recording what had happened, with a minimum of comment, and with neither ostentatious approval or disapproval. Theirs was the ideal which Henry Adams later found so futile: "To satisfy himself whether, by the severest process of stating, with the least possible comment, such facts as seemed sure, in such order as seemed rigorously consequent, he could fix for a familiar moment a necessary sequence of human movement." (*The Education of Henry Adams,* p. 382.)

There was bound to be a reaction away from this austere principle, especially as so few of its protagonists actually lived up to it. The Victorian era, which in Germany saw the triumph of historicism, was also the era of morality, of moral preaching in law and in economics, in politics and in history, as in art and in literature. It is difficult to know whether such historians as Froude in England, Michelet in France, Treitschke in Germany or Motley in America considered themselves primarily ethical leaders or historical scholars; in fact they did not distinguish sharply between the two roles. "The eternal truths and rights of things," said James Anthony Froude in his Inaugural Address as Rector of St. Andrews University, "exist independent of our thoughts or wishes, fixed as mathematics, inherent in the nature of man and the world."

To the American, John L. Motley, historian of the heroic struggle of the Dutch against the Spanish rulers, and of the creation of a United Netherlands, this was the story of the struggle of Protestantism against Catholicism, of the principle of liberty against the principle of tyranny. Motley did not hesitate to pronounce moral judgment; listen to his final verdict on Philip II of Spain:

There have been few men known to history who have been able to accomplish by their own exertions so vast an amount of evil as the king who had just died. If Philip possessed a single virtue it has eluded the conscientious research of the writer of these pages. If there are vices—as possibly there are—from which he was exempt, it is because it is not permitted to human nature to attain perfection even in evil. The only plausible explanation—for palliation there is none—of his infamous career is that the man really believed himself not a king but a God. He was placed so high above his fellow creatures as, in good faith perhaps, to believe himself incapable of doing wrong; so that, whether indulging his passions or enforcing throughout the world his religious and political dogmas, he was ever conscious of embodying divine inspirations and elemental laws. When providing for the assassination of a monarch, or commanding the massacre of a townful of Protestants; when trampling on every oath by which a human being can bind himself when laying desolate with fire and sword during more than a generation the provinces which he had inherited as his private property or in carefully maintaining the flames of civil war in foreign kingdoms which he hoped to acquire; while maintaining over all Christendom a gigantic system of bribery, corruption and espionage . . . he ever felt that these base or bloody deeds were not crimes, but the simple will of the godhead of which he was a portion. (*United Netherlands,* New York, 1868, V, pp. 74–75.)

And, in case his readers might think that he had stepped out of his province in thus condemning the Spanish monarch, Motley added a word on the responsibility of the historian:

> When an humble malefactor is brought before an ordinary court of justice, it is not often, in any age or country, that he escapes the pillory or the gallows because, from his own point of view, his actions, instead of being criminal, have been commendable, and because the multitude and continuity of his offenses prove him to have been sincere. And because anointed monarchs are amenable to no human tribunal, save to that terrible assize which the People, bursting its chain from time to time in the course of the ages, sets up for the trial of its oppressors, and which is called Revolution, it is the more important for the great interests of humanity that before the judgment-seat of History a crown should be no protection to its wearer. There is no plea to the jurisdiction of history, if history be true to itself.
>
> As for the royal criminal called Philip II, his life is his arraignment, and these volumes will have been written in vain if a specification is now required. (*Ibid.*, p. 79.)

In a Carlyle or a Motley moral judgment was a form of self-indulgence. But there was more to it than this, there was high Duty! The clearest and most persuasive statement of the moral function of the historian came from Lord Acton himself. In 1895 Lord Acton was appointed Regius Professor of History at Cambridge University. In his Inaugural Address he exhorted his listeners, and all students of history,

> never to debase the moral currency or to lower the standards of rectitude, but to try others by the final maxim that governs your own lives, and to suffer no man and no cause to escape the undying penalty which history has the power to inflict on wrong. The plea in extenuation of guilt and mitigation of punishment is perpetual. At every step we are met by arguments which go to excuse, to palliate, to confound right and wrong and reduce the just man to the level of the reprobate. . . Opinions alter, manners change, creeds rise and fall, but the moral law is written on the tablets of eternity.

"We have the power," he concluded, ". . . to learn from undisguised and genuine records to look with remorse upon the past, and to the future with assured hope of better things; bearing this in mind, that if we lower our standard in History, we cannot uphold it in Church or State."

We cannot glibly ascribe Acton's philosophy to his Catholicism; he was, after all, not a very orthodox Catholic. Such diverse contemporary historians as Veronica Wedgwood, Isaiah Berlin, and Arnold Toynbee—none of them Catholic—all come out for the obligation, or the necessity, of moral judgment in history. Thus Miss Wedgwood, who has done so much to illuminate the great political and religious issues that stirred England in the seventeenth century, warns us against

> the confusion into which historians fall when they make allowances for "the standards of the age." Their intention is to understand and be just to the past, but the result in the long run may be unfair to the present, because this outlook steadily and stealthily fosters the conviction that nothing is good or bad in itself, but only in relation to its surroundings. . . The aspiration to understand and to forgive is noble and valid in personal relationships between the living but [she concludes] the application of the principle of . . . forgiveness to historical personages is a sentimental fallacy. (*Truth and Opinion,* New York: The Macmillan Company, 1965, pp. 48–49.)

Arnold Toynbee, who has concerned himself more consistently with the universal and the eternal than any other modern historian, has remained throughout his distinguished career a Christian moralist, ready to judge the quick and the dead; his assertion that the expulsion of the Arabs from Palestine by the Israelis was no less a crime than the Nazi murder of some six million Jews precipitated an international controversy.

All of this constitutes what might be called a moral argument in favor of moral judgment. The moral laws are universal and timeless; murder is always murder and betrayal is always betrayal, cruelty and intolerance are always the same, the historian cannot stand above the moral laws, or stand aside from them, but must acknowledge them and participate in them and apply them. If he does not, he will fail the cause of morality—and of History as well—and forfeit the confidence and respect of his peers.

There is, however, another and perhaps more persuasive argument for moral judgment in history, one that rests not so much on moral as on psychological grounds. It is this: that the historian cannot, in any event, help himself, and that he might as well acknowledge what is inherent and implicit in his condition. He is, after all, a creature of his time, his society, his faith. Even if he resolutely refrains from overt moral judgment, he will surely be guilty of covert judgment: his choice of subject, his selection of facts, his very vocabulary, will betray him. How much better, then, how much fairer and more honest, to acknowledge his position in advance; how much better to call his book—it is Charles A. Beard who makes the point—*An Economic Interpretation of the Constitution* rather than to fall back on a title like *The Making of the Constitution,* one which "does not advise the reader at the outset concerning the upshot to be expected." History is not a science, and the historian is not a scientist. "The supreme command," therefore, "is that he must cast off his servitude to the assumptions of natural science and return to his own subject matter—to history as actuality."

This is the argument, too, of the distinguished Oxford philosopher, Sir Isaiah Berlin, who sees in the passion for scientific impartiality yet another expression of the misguided and pernicious belief that history is a science. "The case against the notion of historical objectivity," he writes, "is like the case against international law, or international morality; that it does not exist." And he adds the warning that:

> Except on the assumption that history must deal with human beings purely as material objects in space, must, in short, be behaviourist—its method can scarcely be assimilated to the standards of an exact natural science. The invocation to historians to suppress even that minimal degree of moral or psychological evaluation which is necessarily involved in viewing human beings as creatures with purposes and motives . . . seems to me to rest upon a confusion of the aims and methods of the humane studies with those of natural science. It is one of the greatest and most destructive fallacies of the last hundred years. (*Historical Inevitability,* Oxford, Oxford University Press, 1954, pp. 52–53.)

But the stout champions of moral judgment do not have things all their own way. Not at all. Here comes a whole phalanx of historians with a formidable arsenal of counter-arguments.

First, while it is true that history tries to observe something like historical "due process," it cannot in the nature of the case do so. The past is not there to defend itself. We cannot recall the witnesses, put them on the stand, question and cross-examine them. It is difficult enough to render a moral verdict on anything so recent as, let us say, Hoover's dispersion of the "bonus army," or the conduct of the Vichy government, or the resort to the atomic weapon at Hiroshima; how much more difficult, then, to sit in judgment on the character of Alcibiades, the justification for the murder of Caesar, the conduct of the Norman invaders of England, or of the Spanish conquistadores.

Second, while technical judgment is essential, in the law, in the civil service, in the university, in athletics, if society is to function, such judgment does not pretend to be moral but professional. A university professor who permitted his moral views of a candidate to dictate his grades, a referee whose decisions were based on moral considerations, even a judge who allowed his private moral convictions to influence his decisions on questions of contracts, wills, liability, or bankruptcy proceedings, would be regarded as not only incompetent but expendable. There are reasonably clear standards for such practical judgments as society requires—laws, rules, tests—but as parents, psychiatrists, and priests so well know, moral judgments present questions of labyrinthine complexity even when all the relevant evidence appears to be available. Where history is concerned, the conduct of men or of nations in past centuries, all the relevant evidence is never available, and there are no universal standards. What the historian does, when he judges, is merely to identify his own "can't-help-but-believes" with eternal verities. Herodotus made this point twenty-five centuries ago: When Darius was upon the throne, he summoned

> into his presence the Hellenes at his court and asked them for what price they would consent to make a meal of their fathers when they died. The Hellenes replied that all the money in the World would not induce them to do such a thing, whereupon Darius summoned the Callatian Indians, who do eat their parents, and asked them (in the presence of the Hellenes, who were kept informed, through an interpreter, of the tenour of the conversation) for what price they would be willing to burn their fathers when they died. The Indians shrieked aloud and begged him not to pursue an unmentionable subject—a story which illustrates the habitual attitude of Mankind towards this question, and which, in my opinion, justifies Pindar's poetic aphorism that "Custom is king of all."

Justice Holmes made the point with even greater succinctness. "I prefer champagne to ditch-water," he said, "but I see no reason to suppose the cosmos does."

If history "tells us" anything, it tells us that standards, values, and principles have varied greatly from age to age and from society to society; indeed, that they have varied greatly from one generation to another within the same society. Popes chosen for their learning and their virtue were certain that morality required that they put down heresies with fire and sword, cruelty and torture; sixteenth century Europeans had no compunction about killing Indians, because the Indians had no souls; learned and upright Puritans readily sent witches to their death; and nineteenth century Christians in the American South regarded slavery as a blessing. The Hellenes of whom Herodotus tells us were no more shocked at the notion of eating their dead fathers than we are at Hellenic notions of love. Consider, for example, Plato's defense of a practice which most of our contemporaries regard not only as immoral but as pernicious, and which our military and civil authorities combat with sleepless zeal:

> I cannot say what greater benefit can fall to the lot of a young man than a virtuous lover and to the lover than a beloved youth. . . If then there were any means whereby a state or army could be formed of lovers and favorites, they would administer affairs better than all others, provided they abstain from all disgraceful deeds and compete with one another

in honest rivalry, and such men, together with others like them, though few in number, so to speak would conquer the world. (*Symposium,* p. 178.)

A problem which has confronted, and perplexed, American historians for a hundred years is slavery. Surely if anything is wrong, slavery is wrong. No social institution more deeply offends our moral sensibilities than this; no other collective experience induces in us a comparable sense of shame. Slavery, we are all agreed, corrupts alike the slave and the master; slavery corrupts the body politic, the poison still infects us.

This is the vocabulary of morality, and it is this vocabulary which we invoke, almost instinctively, whenever we discuss what was long euphemistically called the "peculiar institution."

Yet when we come to pronounce judgment on slavery we are met, at the very threshold, with the most intransigent consideration—that generation after generation of good, humane, Christian men and women not only accepted it, but considered it a blessing. What are we to say when confronted by the fact—a formidable body of evidence permits us to use that word—that our own forebears, only two or three generations back, embraced slavery, rejoiced in it, fought to defend it, and gave up their lives confident that they were dying in a good cause.

Clearly, we cannot fall back on the simple explanation that all these men and women—those who owned slaves and those who sustained the slave system—were bad. These beneficiaries of and defenders of slavery were neither better nor worse than their cousins north of the Mason and Dixon line who had managed to get rid of the "peculiar institution" one or two generations earlier; they were neither better nor worse than we are. Whatever may be said, on practical grounds, for the moral righteousness and self-righteousness of Abolitionists who fought slavery, it can be said that no comparable pressures weigh upon us as historians. It is absurd for us to pass moral judgment on slave-holders, absurd to indict a whole people or to banish a whole people to some historical purgatory where they can expiate their sins. Lincoln saw this, Lincoln who saw so much. The people of the North and the South, he said in his Second Inaugural Address, "read the same Bible and pray to the same God, and each invokes His aid against the other. It may seem strange that any men should dare to ask a just God's assistance in wringing their bread from the sweat of other men's faces. But let us judge not, that we be not judged."

We can agree now, most of us, that slavery was an unmitigated evil, but we cannot therefrom conclude that those who inherited it, were caught in it and by it, supported it and fought for it, were evil men. What we can say is that but for the grace of God, or the accident of history, we might ourselves have been caught up in slavery, and bound by it, and habituated to accepting it, just as our forebears were. What we can say is that if earlier generations—North and South alike—bore the burden and the guilt of slavery, we have born the burden, and the guilt, of racial discrimination, and that morally there is not much to choose between the two.

Clearly, different generations have different moral standards; it is a form of intellectual arrogance for us to impose ours upon the past. We do not accept ex post facto laws, bills of attainder, or guilt by association in our legal system; we should not apply these concepts or rules retroactively to the past. Far better to refrain from the folly and the vanity of moral righteousness about the past; far better to accept Lincoln's admonition to judge not, that we be not judged. The historian's task is not to judge, but to understand. How did it happen that men dedicated to carrying out the precepts of the Sermon on the Mount could send those who disagreed with them to the stake? How did it happen that men dedicated to the expansion of European civilization could carry fire and sword to the hapless inhabitants of the American continents? How did it happen that men and women who dearly loved their own children and whose daily lives were bound each to each with natural piety could bitterly oppose laws designed to protect little children from the awful burden of work in factory and mine? How did it happen that Christian men and women could look upon slavery as a blessing? How did it happen that a people who boasted a high civilization, who had produced Leibniz and Kant, Beethoven and Mozart, Goethe and Heine, Rilke and Thomas Mann, could stand by while six million Jews were done to death?

Tout comprendre, tout pardonner. But it does not follow that the historian who understands all forgives all. It is the historian's business to "understand"; it is not the historian's business either to condemn or to forgive. He is not God.

For here is a third argument against moral judgment in history—that the historian is not God. He is not called upon to judge the quick or the dead; indeed he is not called upon to judge. If he sets up as a judge he changes the whole pattern of his intellectual and professional role from one dedicated to objective inquiry to one devoted to prosecution or defense. As the distinguished historian of the Russian Revolution, E. H. Carr, observes, the attempt to erect standards of historical judgment "is itself unhistorical and contradicts the very essence of history. It provides a dogmatic answer to questions which the historian is bound, by his vocation, incessantly to ask. The historian who accepts answers in advance to these questions, goes to work with his eyes blindfolded, and, renounces his vocation."

The historian is not God; he is a man and like other men. He confesses most of the failings, responds to most of the pressures, succumbs to most of the temptations that afflict his fellow men. Consciously, or unconsciously, he is almost always taking sides. Can we really trust Carlyle on Cromwell, or Motley on Philip II, or Charles A. Beard on the causes of the Civil War or Vernon Parrington on John Marshall? Can we trust either Macaulay or Winston Churchill to write impartially about the Duke of Marlborough? Can we trust Lord Acton or Benedetto Croce on a subject so close to their hearts as the history of liberty? Clearly we cannot. The historian, like the judge, the priest, or the statesman, is a creature of his race, nationality, religion, class, of his inheritance and his education, and he can never emancipate himself from these formative influences and achieve Olympian impartiality. Where he undertakes to *judge* he does not even have the prop of professional training and traditions to sustain him, as he does when he records and reconstructs. His judgments are, therefore, as Herbert Butterfield has observed, but "pseudo-moral judgments, masquerading as moral ones, mixed and muddy affairs, part prejudice, part political animosity, with a dash of ethical flavoring wildly tossed into the concoction." And because not even a Ranke, not even a Mommsen, not even a Toynbee, can survey the whole of history, his forays into the past are bound to be haphazard and fortuitous as well. For purposes of reconstructing the past, that is not a fatal handicap; others will fill in the gaps. But for purposes of formulating a moral code and applying it systematically and impartially, it is a fatal handicap.

We may, then, accept the findings of the historian in matters of fact—always subject to subsequent revision, to be sure—but why should we accept his conclusions in matters of morality? "I beseech you in the bowels of Christ," wrote Oliver Cromwell in his Letter to the Church of Scotland, "think it possible you may be mistaken." Alas, the historians have so often been mistaken. Over the centuries they have stood ready to pronounce judgments which differ little from the tainted and tarnished judgments of statesmen, soldiers, and priests. Catholic historians have sustained the persecution of Protestant heretics, and Protestant historians looked with equanimity upon the persecution of Catholics. National historians have almost invariably defended and justified the conduct of their own nation and as regularly rendered judgment against the enemies of their nation; more, they have themselves provided the arguments for chauvinistic nationalism, imperialism, and militarism. No wonder that the chief professional preoccupation of the historian in our day is revision!

There is no special dispensation for the historian. He is not exempt from the prejudices, the ambitions, the vanities, the fears, that afflict his fellow men. When he dons his professional robes he is an impressive and sometimes a majestic figure; when he is persuaded to put on the robes of the moral judge, he is as naked as the unhappy Emperor of Hans Andersen's story.

We come then to a fourth consideration, practical rather than philosophical: the futility of moral judgment in history. Surely, say those who insist that the historian be a judge, it is proper that the historian reprobate the Inquisition and exalt tolerance, that he deplore slavery and celebrate freedom, that he execrate Hitler and Nazi genocide and rejoice in the triumph of the forces of liberation. But why should the historian go out of his way to condemn or to praise these things? The assumption behind this expectation is that the reader has no mind of his own, no moral standards, no capacity to exercise judgment; that he is incapable of distinguishing between slavery and freedom, persecution and tolerance, but depends upon the historian to do this for him. Are those mature enough to read serious histories really so obtuse that they cannot draw conclusions from the facts that are submitted to them? Is there really any danger that students will yearn for slavery or rejoice in the Inquisition or admire Philip II or Adolf Hitler if the historian does not bustle in and set them right? Alas, if the reader does not know that Hitler was a moral monster and that the murder of six million Jews was a moral outrage, nothing the historian can say will set him right; if he does not know in his bones that slavery corrupts both slave and master, nothing the historian can say will enlighten him. Is there not, indeed, some danger that if the historian continually usurps the role of judge, the reader may react against his judgments; that if the historian insists on treating his readers as morally incompetent, they may turn away from history altogether to some more mature form of literature?

There is a further consideration, which might be called a plea in abatement. It is this: that the problem of judgment may be trusted to take care of itself. No reader comes wholly unprepared to the contemplation of a chapter of history; he brings with him his own education, his own moral and philosophical outlook. Nor is the student ever confined to a single account of any important chapter of history. We can be confident that historians will differ in their interpretation of the past and that these differences will be available and familiar to readers. Errors will be corrected; wrong opinions will be set right. For every historian who defends British policy in Ireland there will be one to expose it and reprobate it; for every historian who paints slavery in sunlight terms, there will be one to expose its darkness and cruelty; for every historian who places responsibility for the First World War squarely at the door of the Germans, there will be one ready to make clear that it was the Russians or the French who were really to blame. Let the historian learn humility: the reader is not dependent upon him for the whole of his history; he is not dependent upon him for moral instruction.

That is what the great Italian historical philosopher Benedetto Croce meant when he wrote that "those who, on the plea of narrating history, bustle about as judges, condemning here and giving absolution there, because they think that this is the office of history, are generally recognized as devoid of historical sense."

One final observation is appropriate. We should not confuse moral with professional judgment. In the field of his professional competence the scholar has the same obligation as the judge, the teacher, the physician, the architect. The judge who pronounces sentence, the teacher who gives a grade, the physician who diagnoses an illness, the architect who condemns a building, is not indulging in moral but exercising professional judgment. So the historian who, after painstaking study of all available evidence, and after cleansing himself of all the perilous stuff which might distort his vision, concludes that Lee did right to surrender at Appomattox rather than fight it out in the west, that Roosevelt was not responsible for the attack on Pearl Harbor, that the conduct of the Crimean War was characterized by criminal folly, that the violation of Belgian neutrality in 1914 was an error of the first magnitude, that Cavour rather than Garibaldi deserves credit for Italian unification, that Shakespeare and not Bacon wrote *Hamlet,* that only the stone and not the inscription on the Kensington rune stone is genuine, and that the Protocols of Zion are forgeries, is performing his professional duty. He may be mistaken—but so may the judge, the teacher, the physician— that is a chance society takes. His judgments may have moral overtones —it is difficult to keep those out, and we have learned to discount them. But if it is exasperating to find a Carlyle or a Motley laying down the moral laws for us, it is equally exasperating to discover that when you lay all the scholarly investigators of a subject end to end, they do not reach a conclusion.

History as Law and as Philosophy
chapter five

THE USE OF HISTORY

We are all acquainted with the young man who earnestly assures us, with a mixture of vanity and zeal, that he has always "hated history." It is all dates, he tells us, or it is all a lot of rather tiresome problems—the problem of the "fall" of Rome, the problem of the French Revolution, the problem of Secession and Civil War. And it never gets you anywhere; you are no better off when you have finished than when you began.

Some of this attitude may be confidently set down to poor and uninspiring teaching—teaching which never challenged the interest nor excited the imagination of students. Some of it—perhaps a good deal—may be put down to the same kind of uninspired teaching embodied in textbooks in which the authors try to please everybody, avoid the "controversial," ignore the dramatic, concentrate on problems which are never solved or whose solution is of no interest, and, like so many of the novels and dramas of our time, eschew narrative and leave out heroes and villains. Some of it can be ascribed to the individual himself; his inability to respond imaginatively to the drama of the past. In all likelihood he is one of those of whom Wordsworth wrote:

A primrose by the river's brim,
A yellow primrose was to him,
And it was nothing more.

But after we have done all this explaining, there remains a stubborn residuum of intelligent and open-minded students who still find nothing to nourish them in history. They may agree with Gibbon that history is "the register of the follies and misfortunes of mankind," or with Napoleon that it is a "lie agreed upon," or with Carlyle that it is "a great dust-heap," and they do not stop to read those marvellous volumes in which Gibbon recorded the "follies and misfortunes" of man, or discover how Carlyle proved that history was charged with life and passion, nor are they excited by the challenge to separate truth from lies about Napoleon himself.

What are we to say to all this? Why should the young study history? Why should their elders read history, or write it?

That is a question which recurs again and again: What use is history? Let us admit at once that in a practical way history has no use, let us concede that it is not good for anything that can be weighed, measured, or counted. It will not solve problems; it will not guarantee us against the errors of the past; it will not show nations how to avoid wars, or how to win them; it will not provide scientific explanations of depressions or keys to prosperity; it will not contribute in any overt way to progress.

But the same can be said, of course, of many other things which society values and which men cherish. What use, after all, is a Mozart sonata or a painting by Renoir, or a statue by Milles? What use is the cathedral of Siena or the rose windows of Chartres or a novel by Flaubert or a sonnet by Wordsworth? What use, for that matter, are a great many mundane things which society takes for granted and on which it lavishes thought and effort: a baseball game, for example, or a rose garden, or a brocade dress, or a bottle of port?

Happily, a civilized society does not devote all of its thought and effort to things whose usefulness can be statistically demonstrated. There are other criteria than that of usefulness, and other meanings to the term "useful" than those acknowledged by the Thomas Gradgrinds of this world.

History, we can confidently assert, is useful in the sense that art and music, poetry and flowers, religion and philosophy are useful. Without it—as without these—life would be poorer and meaner; without it we should be denied some of those intellectual and moral experiences which give meaning and richness to life. Surely it is no accident that the study of history has been the solace of many of the noblest minds of every generation.

The first and doubtless the richest pleasure of history is that it adds new dimensions to life itself, enormously extending our perspective and enlarging our experience. It permits us to enter vicariously into the past, to project our vision back over thousands of years and enlarge it to embrace all the races of mankind. Through the pages of history we can hear Pericles deliver his Funeral Oration, look with wonder as Scipio and Hannibal lock forces in that desperate field of Zama, trek with the Crusaders to the Holy Land, sail with Columbus past the gates of Hercules and to a new world, sit with Diderot as he edits the En-cyclopédie, share the life of Goethe and Schiller at the little court of Weimar, stand and listen to those stirring debates in those dusty prairie towns which sent Douglas to the Senate and Lincoln to the White House, share the agony of General Lee as he surrenders the Army of Northern Virginia at McLean's Court House, stand beside Winston Churchill as he rallies the people of Britain to their finest hour. History supplies to us all those elements which Henry James thought essential to the life of the mind: density, variety, intricacy, richness, in the pattern of thought and of action, and with it "the sense of the past."

This immense enlargement of experience means, of course, that history provides us with great companions on our journey through life. This is so familiar a consideration that it needs no elaboration. Wherever the historian or biographer has been, he has given new depth and range to our associations. We have but to take down the books and we are admitted to the confidence of Voltaire and Rousseau, Johnson and Boswell, Thomas Jefferson and John Adams, Justice Holmes and William James. We can know them with more of an intimacy than their contempo-raries knew them, for we can read their letters, journals and diaries. This is not just one of the pleasures of history, it is one of the indispensable pleasures of life.

A third, and familiar, pleasure of history is the experience of identi-fying the present with the past, and thus adding a new dimension to places and events. It was Macaulay who observed that "the pleasure of History is analogous in many respects to that produced by foreign travel. The student is transported into a new state of society. He sees new fashions. He hears new modes of expression. His mind is enlarged by contemplating the wide diversities of laws, of morals, and of manners." George Macaulay Trevelyan—himself a grand-nephew of Macaulay— has conjured up this pleasure for us in one of his most glowing passages:

> Places, like books, have an interest or a beauty of association, as well as an absolute or aesthetic beauty. The garden front of St. John's, Oxford, is beautiful to everyone; but for the lover of history its outward charm is blent with the intimate feelings of his own mind, with images of that same college as it was during the Great Civil War. Given over to the use of a Court whose days of royalty were numbered, its walks and quadrangles were filled, as the end came near, with men and women learning to accept sorrow as their lot through life, the ambitious abandon-ing hope of power, the wealthy hardening themselves to embrace poverty, those who loved England preparing to sail for foreign shores, and lovers

to be parted forever. There they strolled through the garden, as the hopeless evenings fell, listening, at the end of all, while the siege guns broke the silence with ominous iteration. Behind the cannon on those low hills to northward were ranked the inexorable men who came to lay their hands on all this beauty, hoping to change it to strength and sterner virtue. And this was the curse of the victors, not to die, but to live, and almost to lose their awful faith in God, when they saw the Restoration, not of the old gaiety, that was too gay for them, and the old loyalty that was too loyal for them, but of corruption and selfishness that had neither country nor king. The sound of the Roundhead cannon has long ago died away, but still the silence of the garden is heavy with unalterable fate, brooding over besiegers and besieged, in such haste to destroy each other and permit only the vile to survive. St. John's College is not mere stone and mortar, tastefully compiled, but an appropriate and mournful witness between those who see it now and those by whom it once was seen. (*Clio, A Muse and Other Essays,* New York, 1913, p. 26.)

Everyone who has visited historic towns, in the Old World or the New, knows that when he looks at them through the eyes of history they cease to be museum pieces and pulse with life and with vigor. Nestling between its ancient hills, bisected by the gleaming Arno, its domes and towers piercing the skies, Florence is beautiful to the eyes of even the purblind. But how it springs into life when we people its piazzas and narrow streets with the men and women of the past: when we conjure up the spectacle of Savonarola burned at the stake in the great Piazza de la Signoria where the mighty David now stands; Bruneleschi erecting the giant Duomo; Ghiberti carving the great bronze doors of the Baptistry, a lifetime work, this; Giotto and Fra Filippo Lippi and Raphael and Leonardo and Michelangelo painting those pictures which now hang in such lavish profusion from the glittering walls of the Uffizi and the Pitti palaces; Machiavelli pondering the history of the condottieri while he writes the *Prince,* and Galileo seeing a new universe through his telescope and opening up a new universe of the mind as well. Did ever a city boast a comparable galaxy of genius; did ever a city publish itself more generously in its monuments, or impress itself more richly on the eye and on the mind?

Nor is it only the great centers of art and letters, like Florence or Venice or Salzburg, that take on new dimensions when seen through the eyes of history; the same miracle transforms even the most modest of towns. Henry James observed, somewhat condescendingly, that Emerson had "dwelt for fifty years within the undecorated walls of his youth"; but to Emerson those rooms were redolent of the past, as was the little village of Concord. And as for Hawthorne, how, wrote James, could he have found materials for his stories, living where he did, where "the coldness, the thinness, the blankness . . . present themselves so vividly that our foremost feeling is that of compassion for a romancer looking for subjects in such a field." But Hawthorne himself looked out of his attic window on a Salem rich in history and tradition and found in it the ingredients for *The Scarlet Letter* and *The House of Seven Gables,* and a dozen other stories that are a precious part of our literature.

Consider the little town of Salem in Massachusetts, now no more than a suburb of Boston. It is a lovely town in its own right, there by the sea and the rocks, its handsome old houses still standing sedately along Chestnut and Federal Streets. As we look at it through the eyes of history we conjure up a straggling village busy with fishing and with theological disputes and remember that Roger Williams preached here those heresies which brought him banishment from the Bay Colony, and so too Mistress Anne Hutchinson. We look at Gallows Hill and recall the dark and terrifying story of Salem witchcraft which haunted Nathaniel Hawthorne, who grew up here, and whose spirit still broods over the town. We recreate it in its heyday, when its captains sailed all the waters of the globe and its flag was thought to be the flag of an independent nation, and the spoils and rewards of the China trade glittered in every drawing room. For at the turn of the century Salem was like one of the famous city states of Italy—Florence or Venice or Pisa. It had its own architects, like Samuel McIntyre who built the stately mansions of the sea captains and the merchant princes, mansions which still stand; its own preachers, like the famous William Bentley of the East Church, reputed to be the most learned man in America; its own jurists, like Samuel Putnam and Samuel Sewall who became Chief Justices of the Commonwealth, and Joseph Story who joined the Supreme Court of the United States at thirty-two. Samuel Bowditch was a boy here, watching the sailing ships come in to India Wharf and learning celestial mathematics and navigation from a library which had been captured from a British ship during the War for Independence; he sailed on a Salem merchantman, and grew up to write the *Practical Navigator.* So was George Crowninshield who built the magnificent Cleopatra's Barge and sailed it through the Mediterranean, and the dour Timothy Pickering who lived in the oldest house in town—which still stands— and grew up to be the most reactionary politician in the country; so too the astonishing Benjamin Thompson who grew up to be Count Rumford of the Holy Roman Empire and to live in state in Munich and found the Royal Institution in London, and so too William Prescott who played as a boy along India Wharf and Derby Wharf, and swam in the cold waters of the harbor and picnicked on Hog Island, and who became the historian of Mexico and of Peru.—Then another generation, and Salem entered its long decline, its harbors silted up and its wharfs falling into decay and grass growing up between the cobblestones of its ancient streets, while the paint peeled off the proud McIntyre houses. It is all there—in Nathaniel Hawthorne's stories, in the reminiscences of Joseph Story and Rufus Choate, in the historical romances by Joseph Hergesheimer and Esther Forbes, so faithful to the spirit and the reality of the old town—all there for us to recapture through the pages of history.

Needless to say, all this makes great demands upon the imagination, the imagination of the historian and of the student alike. "At bottom," George Macaulay Trevelyan has said, "the appeal of history is imaginative," and he gives us, as an example of this, one of Carlyle's recreations of the past—it is in his essay on Boswell's Johnson:

Rough Samuel and sleek wheedling James *were*, and *are not*. Their Life and whole personal Environment has melted into air. The Mitre Tavern still stands in Fleet Street; but where now is its scot-and-lot paying, beef-and-ale loving, cocked-hatted, pot-bellied Landlord; its rosy-faced assiduous Landlady, with all her shining brass-pans, waxed tables, well-filled larder-shelves; her cooks and bootjacks, and errand boys and watery-mouthed hangers-on? Gone! Gone! The becking Waiter, who, with wreathed smiles, was wont to spread for Samuel and Bozzy their supper of the gods, has long since pocketed his last sixpence; and vanished, sixpences and all, like a ghost at cock-crowing. The Bottles they drank out of are all broken, the Chairs they sat on all rotted and burnt; the very Knives and Forks they ate with have rusted to the heart, and become brown oxide of iron, and mingled with the indiscriminate clay. All, all has vanished; in very deed and truth, like that baseless fabric of Prospero's air-vision. Of the Mitre Tavern nothing but the bare walls remain there; of London, of England, of the World, nothing but the bare walls remain; and these also decaying (were they of adamant), only slower. The mysterious River of Existence rushes on; a new Billow thereof has arrived, and lashes wildly as ever round the old embankments; but the former Billow with its loud, mad eddyings, where is it?—Where?—

Now this *Book* of Boswell's, this is precisely a revocation of the edict of Destiny; so that Time shall not utterly, not so soon by several centuries, have dominion over us. (*Critical Essays*, p. 4.)

A dangerous thing, this, for once we introduce the element of imagination we imperil the integrity of the historical record. Yet how can we possibly exclude it? What is history, after all, without imagination? Imagination comes to our aid at every moment; it is what permits us to clothe the bare bones of history with life. It throws a glow over the most impersonal, the dullest, of the data of history. It infuses even a statistical table with color and life: who can read the statistics of the population growth of the western territories and states of the United States in the nineteenth century without seeing, in his mind's eye, the Conestoga wagon, and the canal boats on the Erie Canal, the railroad puffing its way across the Appalachians, weather-beaten men with their wives and children and cattle, beating out a trail to Oregon or to the Mormon utopia at the Great Salt Lake?

Imagination brings home to us that the names in the history books represent real people, that the decisions which were made involved the same fears and hopes and uncertainties and courage as those which we ourselves make, that Latimer at the stake and Lord Nelson at Trafalgar suffered the same agonies and exaltations which we ourselves experience, that to a man like Robert E. Lee the decision to stay with his state was no abstract "problem" of secession, but just such a spiritual and moral crisis as would plunge us into despair if we confronted it today. Alas, many historians are like the preacher of whom Emerson writes:

> A snow-storm was falling around us. The snow-storm was real, the preacher merely spectral, and the eye felt the sad contrast in looking at him, and then, out of the window behind him into the beautiful meteor of the snow. He had lived in vain. He had no one word intimating that he had laughed or wept, was married or in love, had been commended, or cheated, or chagrined. If he had ever lived and acted, we were none the wiser for it. The capital secret of his profession, namely to convert life into truth, he had not learned. . . This man had ploughed and planted and talked and bought and sold; he had read books; he had eaten and drunken; his head aches, his heart throbs; he smiles and suffers; yet was there not a surmise, a hint, in all the discourse, that he had ever lived at all. (Divinity School Address, July 15, 1838.)

It might be thought that imagination like—let us say—an ear for music, is something you either have or have not. If you have it, well and good; if not, there is nothing to be done about it. But the imagination, like a taste for music, or for painting, can be cultivated. How can the historical imagination be cultivated? It can be cultivated through drama and poetry. Shakespeare suffused the stuff of history with his glorious imagination; no wonder Winston Churchill said that he had learned all of his English history out of Shakespeare! How history comes alive in the novels of Walter Scott—such varied historians as Prescott and Carlyle and Trevelyan have acknowledged his inspiration. With what insight does Wordsworth read its moral lessons, in the sonnet "On the Extinction of the Venetian Republic," for example, or in "To Toussaint L'Ouverture," or in *The Prelude*. Imagination can be cultivated, too, by the study of art and architecture. Who can wander through the National Portrait Gallery in London and not feel stirred by the spectacle of these men and women who have made England; how exhilarating to visit such great Palladian palaces as the Villa Rotonda and the Villa Malcontenta outside Vicenza, and to see Jefferson's Monticello emerge out of these models.

This does not exhaust the pleasures of history; they are, indeed, inexhaustible. We may, without too gross an impropriety paraphrase Dr. Johnson's observation on London, that anyone who is tired of history is tired of life.

Can we go beyond the pleasures of history to Laws of History, or even to the Philosophy of History? That all depends on what you mean by "laws" and by "philosophy."

CAUSATION IN HISTORY

One of the liveliest pleasures of history is that, more continuously and more persuasively than almost any other study, it nourishes and enlists the reflective faculties. Nowhere are those faculties more busily engaged than in seeking for causes.

"Happy is he who knows the causes of things." But if this is true then it can be said that historians are forever pursuing happiness, but never quite attaining it. The search for the causes of things is, and has long been, the chief preoccupation of thoughtful historians. No self-respecting modern historian is content merely with recording what happened; he wants to explain why it happened. Of all problems of history, causation is the most urgent, the most fascinating, and the most baffling.

Why did history turn out the way it did? Why were the Chinese ahead of the West in civilization; why did civilization flourish so spectacularly in Greece at a time when most of Europe was lost in what we think of as barbarism; why were Europeans so far in advance of Americans for so many centuries? Why did the Roman Empire "decline and fall"; why were the Moslems able to conquer so much of Europe, and why did Moslem power ebb? What explains the amazing vitality of the Vikings and then of the Norsemen who swarmed over seas and over land, and carried their culture to the shores of Ireland and France and Sicily, and then fell back into obscurity? How did it happen that a little fog-bound island off the north coast of Europe came to be one of the greatest of world powers, and that the English language—of all unlikely languages—came to be spoken from London to Singapore and from Toronto to the Cape of Good Hope? Why did the American colonies break away from the Mother Country, and why were they successful in their revolution; why did the Southern States break away from the American Union and why was their revolution unsuccessful? Why did British America become two great countries, while Latin America fragmented into more than twenty? Why do only English-speaking peoples have a two-party system while all others have a one- or a multi-party system? What caused the two great wars of the twentieth century; what explains the spread and the triumphs of Communism? How explain the change in styles, from classical to romantic, from romantic to modern? How explain the change in moral standards from age to age—the changing attitude towards slavery, for example, or towards child labor, or towards sex?

For over two thousand years philosophers and historians have tried to answer these and similar questions about the course of history, though it is only in the last two or three centuries that the inquiry has been both open-minded and independent. Socrates, in one of the most famous of his discourses, asserted the validity of inquiry: "That we shall be better and braver and less helpless if we think that we ought to enquire than we should have been if we indulged in the idle fancy that there was no knowing and no use in seeking to know what we do not know—that is a theme upon which I am ready to fight in word and deed to the utmost of my power."

Yet most ancient historians did, in fact, indulge in something very like "idle fancy." The great Greek and Roman historians rarely inquired into the causes of things; it was enough for them that whatever happened was bound to happen, that it was all in the hands of the gods or of fate:

> The things men looked for cometh not,
> And a path there is where no man thought—
> So hath it fallen here.

Even so great an historian as Thucydides does not seek the deeper causes of the Peloponnesian War or the defeat of Athens, nor does a moralist like Plutarch inquire into the explanation for the virtues and the vices which he describes.

Christian historians, too, had an easy time of it. Everything that happened in history, from the sparrow that fell to the earth to the fall of empires, had a cause: it was all the working out of a divine plan. St. Augustine had made this clear, once and for all, in *The City of God,* and thereafter it was accepted without serious question. It is hard for us to realize, now, how this simplistic theory dominated historical thinking for more than a thousand years, how it persisted, even, well past the Renaissance and Reformation and down to the Age of Reason. Thus it was in the seventeenth century that the great French historian, Jacques Bossuet prepared his *Discourses on Universal History* to demonstrate that the whole course of history was but the working out of a divine plan which happened, also, to be the plan of the Catholic popes. And at almost the same time, Bossuet's American contemporary, Edward Johnson, explained the planting of the Bay Colony under the title *The Wonder-Working Providence of Sion's Saviour in New England.* Or consider the great debate over the meaning and the explanation of America which raged from the fifteenth to the eighteenth centuries. How explain the New World? How explain its primitive state, the backwardness of its native races, the absence of organized society, or government? Every historian and philosopher who addressed himself to this problem started with the Flood, postulating for the New World a later Flood or a greater Flood or a series of Floods; all, too, with few exceptions, took for granted that mankind in every continent was descended from a common set of ancestors, Adam and Eve.

The mental habit of ascribing historical events, great and small, to the caprice of the gods or to the inscrutable will of God, persisted even into the eighteenth century: thus the popularity of cyclical theories of history or of what might be called the "ebb and flow" theory, as illustrated by *The Grandeur and Decadence of Rome,* or the *Decline and Fall of the Roman Empire, Westward the Star of Empire,* and other books with titles of a like nature. So, too, did the habit of acknowledging the authority of impersonal law, only now it was secular, not divine law, now it was "the law of Nature" as well as of "Nature's God." This was the Newtonian theory applied to the affairs of men, and it had the immense advantage of making history not only a secular but a rational affair. Soon all the historians and philosophers were explaining history in terms of Nature, and in one way or another this has persisted down to our own time. The eighteenth century concept of Nature and Nature's law was, however, very different from ours: Nature was orderly, rational, and, in a curious way, anthropocentric. The universe, as men knew it, was ruled by Law that operated harmoniously and implacably, like some great mechanism; as men were part of the universe, they, too, were subject to universal law. Oddly enough this did not turn out to be deterministic in any malign sense. For the laws which controlled the universe were harmonious and rational. That meant that they applied to society and government as well as to the courses of the stars or the ebb and flow of the tides, and it meant that they could be apprehended and adopted by the reason of man. If men could but conform to these laws of Nature instead of ignoring them or flouting them, the miseries and agonies that had so long afflicted man would disappear, and peace, prosperity, and progress would usher in a millenium.

Curiously enough, though the faith in Reason evaporated, reliance on Force persisted in a more sophisticated form down to our own time. Montesquieu had argued the importance of "climate" in history—a term which he used much as we would use the term "environment," and since his day climate or geography has been one of the most popular of all explanations of history. The Abbé Raynal used it to explain the backwardness of the Americas; and after him a host of scholars and scientists as diverse as Alexander von Humboldt and Henry T. Buckle, Richard Green and Friedrich Raetzel, Frederick Jackson Turner and Brooks Adams celebrated the predominant role of climate and geography in guiding the destinies of man. But climate and geography were by no means the only impersonal forces which won the allegiance of historians. Karl Marx founded a school of history, and not of history alone, which interpreted most of the activities and ideas of men in terms of economic interests and forces. Admiral Mahan worshipped sea power as a kind of brooding omniscience in history; Henry Adams insisted quite simply on force—first—and for many centuries—the force of religion, then, in modern times, coal, steam, and electricity as symbolized in the dynamo. "The historians' business," wrote Henry Adams, "was to follow the track of energy" wherever it led, and that is what he did, until he came at last to radium and to atomic power. "Power leaped from every atom, and enough of it to supply the stellar universe showed itself running to waste at every pore of matter. Man could no longer hold it off. Forces grasped his wrist and flung him about as though he had hold of a live wire." (*The Education of Henry Adams*, p. 494.)

The "forces of the stellar universe" were impersonal and aimless; if history was indeed controlled by such forces, there was no possibility of reducing it to law—just what Adams concluded when he somewhat perversely hit upon the law of the dissipation of energy as the sovereign law of history. But the eighteenth century had invented and the nineteenth had perfected a new and more benign force. Progress was the new idea and the new force; progress first within the framework of Natural Law and then within the framework of Evolution. Turgot had announced it in a memorable address in 1750; the Encyclopaedists had embraced it, and with Condorcet it became well-nigh official. We are all children of the Age of Progress, all heirs to the belief that

> through the ages one increasing purpose runs,
> And the thoughts of men are widened with the process of the suns,
> (Tennyson, "Locksley Hall")

and it is unnecessary to elaborate upon anything so familiar.

The doctrine of progress was confirmed by faith rather than by observation, and sometimes—as Voltaire made clear in *Candide* or Dr. Johnson in *Rasselas*—faith gave way to scepticism. It lacked historical support—had there really been progress in the oldest societies such as China or Egypt or Greece?—and it lacked scientific support, as well. How fortunate, then, that the doctrine of evolution appeared to provide it with the strongest scientific support, at least the doctrine of evolution according to Herbert Spencer. For Spencer made clear that the great, transcendent laws of organic evolution which regulated the animal world, regulated the world of man as well. As evolution assured the survival of the fittest in the world of Nature, so it guaranteed that man, too, would progress towards perfection by the elimination of all imperfections. "Progress is not an accident," said Spencer, "but a necessity. It is a part of Nature." And his American disciple, John Fiske, wrote raptly that "The creation of Man is the goal towards which Nature tended from the beginning. Not the production of any higher creature, but the perfecting of Humanity, is to be the glorious consummation of Nature's long and tedious work."

All this was gratifying enough, but as an explanation of history it was not very helpful. For to be told, when we ask why Rome declined, or why the Spanish Armada foundered, or why the Confederacy lost the Civil War, that it was all in harmony with the law of Progress, or that it was part of Evolution, leaves us pretty much where we were in the beginning. Granted Progress, granted Evolution, why should they manifest themselves in one way rather than in another? Was the decline of the Roman Empire progress? Is it certain that Britain and not Spain was destined to be the beneficiary of the evolutionary process?

No, the search for an explanation could not be satisfied that easily. If we were to explain the past, if we were to predict the future, we needed something at once more rigorous and more specific than the windy doctrine of progress or the impersonal doctrine of evolution. Mathematics, biology, chemistry, physics, these things had provided laws which explained so much that had heretofore been mysterious; surely history, too, could provide laws which would explain the past and illuminate the future. So said Auguste Comte, in France, who worked out an elaborate scheme of the social sciences; so said Herbert Spencer in England, who created a science of society on the basis of biology and anthropology and psychology; so said the American John Fiske whose *Outlines of Cosmic Philosophy* drew on the whole body of social and philosophical thought to find the laws which regulated the moral world, and whose many histories proved that these laws had operated in America from the beginning. Other social sciences boasted laws— Malthus' law of population growth, Gresham's law in economics, Ferdinand LaSalle's law of wages, Henry Buckle's law of geography, which was "one glorious principle of universal and undeviating regularity"— why should not history, too, have her laws?

LAWS IN HISTORY

"Four out of five students who are living today," wrote Henry Adams some sixty years ago, have, in the course of their work, felt that they stood on the brink of a great generalization that would reduce history under a law as clear as the laws which govern the material world. . . . He seemed to have it, as the Spanish say, in his ink stand. Scores of times he must have dropped his pen to think how one short step, one sudden inspiration, would show all human knowledge; how in these thickest forests of history, one corner turned, one faint trail struck, would bring him on the high road of science.

Alas, when Adams himself hit on a law—it was the law of entropy, or the degradation of energy—it did not clear a way through thickest forests, but put up a permanent barrier to further historical research. Twenty years later Edward P. Cheyney sounded the same note:

> I look forward [he said in his Presidential Address to the American Historical Association in 1923] to some future meeting of this Association when the search for the laws of History and their application will have become the principal part of their procedure. . . . The most conspicuous part on the program will be assigned to some gifted young historical thinker who, quite properly disregarding the earlier and crude efforts of his predecessors, will propound and demonstrate to the satisfaction of all his colleagues, some new and far-reaching law or laws of history.

Alas, again, for human hopes; forty years later the sessions of the Historical Association were given over almost exclusively to "technical history," and philosophical speculations were looked upon with disfavor.

Professor Cheyney himself propounded six "laws of history" and it may be useful to recite them, for they reveal, as well as anything of their kind, some of the difficulties inherent in the formulation of such laws. They are: 1. The law of continuity; 2. The law of mutability; 3. The law of interdependence; 4. The law of democracy; 5. The law of the necessity for free consent; 6. The law of moral progress. Now it can be said of these—as of almost every attempt to formulate laws of history— that either they do not deal with history, but with life in general, or that they are not laws but expressions of hope and of faith. Take, for example, Cheyney's law of continuity. If this means that we have constructed an historical chronology and that in this chronology one event appears to follow another, then it is valid but meaningless. If it means that everything that happens grows out of some antecedent cause which we can discover, then it is not so. The voyages of Columbus and the discovery of America doubtless grew out of a complex of antecedent causes which yield a logical pattern, but can it be said that the destruction of the Aztec and the Inca empires grew out of recognizable causes and followed a pattern which the natives of Mexico and Peru would have regarded as logical? Scholars who trace the history of Negro slavery in America construct a neat and logical pattern which almost makes us think that slavery was inevitable, but is there a comparable logic which would persuade Africans kidnapped and transported to America that slavery was inevitable for them? One major trouble with the principle of continuity and of causation is that it assumes a single line of continuity, a single chain of causes, instead of a hundred or a thousand.

Or consider Cheyney's law of mutability: that nothing is permanent in history. But that is not a law of history, it is a law of life, and poets and moralists had proclaimed it more than two thousand years before Cheyney took it over for history. What is important—and what the historian wants to know—is that some things appear to be more permanent than others. Which seem to be more permanent, and why? To this urgent question the law of mutability says nothing. It is as if we should submit, as a "law" of history, that all men are mortal and that all flesh is grass.

And what of Cheyney's other laws—democracy, liberty, morality? Clearly these are the formulations of a Victorian liberal. How many Chinese or Russian historians would subscribe to the "law" of democracy; how many American Negroes would subscribe to the "law" of liberty; how many German Jews would endorse the "law" of moral progress, or for that matter how many of the survivors of Hiroshima or of Dresden?

Confronted by the seemingly insuperable difficulty of formulating laws or solving the problems of causation, some historians have thrown in the sponge, as it were, and taken refuge in the principle of fortuity. Thus H. A. L. Fisher, whose *History of Europe* is something of a classic, confessed in his preface to that work that:

> One intellectual excitement has been denied me. Men wiser and more learned than I have discovered in history a plot, a rhythm, a predetermined pattern. These harmonies are concealed from me. I can see only one emergency following upon another as wave follows upon wave; only one great fact with respect to which, since it is unique, there can be no generalizations; only one safe rule for the historian: that he should recognize in the development of human destinies the play of the contingent and the unforeseen. (Preface to *A History of Europe*, Boston: Houghton Mifflin Company, 1935–36.)

In its most unsophisticated form this becomes the "Cleopatra's nose" theory of history first stated by no other than Blaise Pascal: "Had Cleopatra's nose been shorter, the whole face of the earth would have been different." Voltaire embraced the same theory, and so too did his friend Frederick the Great: "The older one becomes, the more clearly one sees that King Hazard fashions three-fourths of the events in this miserable world."

"The passion for tidiness," Arthur Schlesinger, Jr., has written, "is the historian's occupational disease." It is, indeed, though we should add in all fairness that it is a kind of historical necessity, as well. Organization always does some violence to the stream of thought or the chaos of conduct that is life—the organization of melody into music, the organization of color into painting, the organization of inspiration into poetry, and of ideas into philosophy, and the organization of facts into history. Granted that history is a record of disorderly conduct; it does not follow that it is to be reported in a disorderely fashion, and it is the mark of a great judge that he is able to bring order and coherence out of conflicting evidence and arguments. History is a jangle of accidents, blunders, surprises and absurdities, and so is our knowledge of it, but if we are to report it at all we must impose some order upon it. Literature is able to compensate for this necessity by falling back on the "stream of consciousness" technique, but history cannot do this.

The danger is that in tidying up history the historian will convey the impression (he may even convince himself!) that everything was tidy from the beginning. A battle, for example, is often a nightmare of blunder and confusion; then the historian comes along and tidies it all up, tells us just how the battle was planned, how the center struck at this moment and the left flank moved in next, how the artillery joined in, or the cavalry charged, and there is your victory, all nicely explained. Or he looks back upon a diplomatic incident, or upon an election, and explains it all very neatly, leaving out all the contingencies, all the unforeseen events, all the hesitations and fears and confusions. He presents us with the logic of some historical *fait accompli*—the Monroe Doctrine, or the Open Door policy, or Truman's Point Four, and we can indeed see how logical it all was; then we learn—as we have recently learned of Point Four, that it was all a series of accidents, and that far from being a deliberate policy it came even to President Truman himself as a happy surprise.

But while we must avoid assuming that history is a kind of chess game with every gambit logical and planned, we must avoid, equally, the other extreme, that of ascribing everything to accident or luck; we must avoid giving too much prominence to untidiness and disorder. For disorder is, in a sense, itself orderly; it is at once a principle of life and a rule of life. Birth is a very disorderly business, but we forget the disorder (or assume that it is taken for granted) and celebrate the birthday. The whole of life is disorderly—our growing-up, our education, our falling in love, our jobs or careers, our relations with friends or enemies. Our societies are disorderly—physically disorderly in their cities, institutionally disorderly in their economies, their politics, their social relationships. Intelligence tries to bring order out of all of this, and thereby to decrease the disorder, or to master it. So, too, in history, the intelligence of the historian is directed to bringing some order out of the chaos of the past.

And there is, too, a further and consoling consideration, that though accidents often change the pace or the pattern of history, they rarely change it in any fundamental way. For the sophisticated historian remembers what is, after all, the common sense of the matter, that there are always enough accidents to go around, and that accidents tend to cancel out, just as the sophisticated spectator at a football game knows that there are enough fumbles to go around and that a particular fumble rarely changes the course of a game, or of a season of games. It is immature and almost perverse to assign too much importance to what we denominate the accidents of history. The wind scattered the Spanish Armada and helped the English destroy it, but that was not the reason why Spain failed to conquer England; Spain had never conquered England, wind or no wind, nor had any other power. Washington surprised the Hessians at Trenton on Christmas of 1776, and the American cause looked up; but that was not the reason the Americans finally won their independence. Even had the Hessians repulsed Washington's ragged troops the Americans would, in all likelihood, have won sooner or later. A Federal soldier picked up Lee's plan of battle for Antietam and took it to McClellan; that was not the reason Lee lost the battle of Antietam or the Confederacy lost the war. Even had Lee won the battle of Antietam it is highly improbable that the Confederacy would have won the war. President Wilson suffered a fateful breakdown on his train outside Wichita, Kansas, in the midst of his crusade for the ratification of the League of Nations, and the League was defeated. But that is not the reason that the Senate rejected the League or that the Republicans won the election of 1920; these things would have come about in any event, regardless of the fate of President Wilson.

Yet in every one of these instances, and in a hundred others which we could readily conjure up, fortuity did play a part, and an important part. It changed things; it meant that some men who might have lived, died; it meant that some battles had to be fought over again; it meant that what we call the course of history was slowed up or speeded up or temporarily deflected.

May we not conclude that fortuity itself is predictable, and that the mature historian takes it into account in his explanations, just as the wise general or statesman takes it into account in his calculations? An earthquake, a drought, the discovery of a new continent, or of gold and silver mines, an epidemic, an assassination, all of these are in a sense fortuitous, yet all of them are in a sense normal, as well, for such as these recur in the history of every country and every century.

Perhaps the most useful lesson the student of history can learn is to avoid oversimplification, and to accept the notion of multiple causation or to resign himself to the fact that as yet we do not know enough to explain the causes of things. To yearn for a single, and usually simple, explanation of the chaotic materials of the past, to search for a single thread in that most tangled of all tangled skeins, is a sign of immaturity. More, it is a practice which encourages dangerous intellectual habits, for it leads, almost inevitably, to a simplistic view of the present as well as of the past. Any historian who invites us to accept some single explanation of the great events of the past excites our distrust; all too often such men find the explanation of prodigious events in some fortuitous occurrence, in some lurid conspiracy, or in some naive observation of character. They tell us that for want of a nail a kingdom was lost; they explain the Reformation in terms of Luther's desire to marry, or the Spanish conquest of Mexico in terms of Cortez' mistress, or the "loss" of China by reference to traitors in the United States Department of State! They are those men of maxims against whom George Eliot has warned us:

> All people of strong, broad sense have an instinctive repugnance to men of maxims; because such people early discover that the mysterious complexity of our life is not to be embraced by maxims, and that to lace ourselves up in formulas of that sort is to repress all the divine promptings and inspirations that spring from a growing insight and sympathy. And the man of maxims is the popular representative of the minds that are guided in their moral judgments solely by general rules, thinking that these will lead them to justice by ready-made patent method, without the trouble of exerting patience, discrimination, impartiality, without any care to assure themselves whether they have the insight that comes from a hardly-earned estimate of temptation, or from a life vivid and intense enough to have created a wide fellow-feeling with all that is human.

THE PHILOSOPHY OF HISTORY

We come then, at the end, to the Philosophy of History. The term itself is ambiguous. It may mean either one of two things, or both of them. It may mean the philosophy which the student brings to the study and the interpretation of history and to which he confidently expects history to conform. Or it may mean, more simply, the philosophy which the student finds in history, and to which he himself will, perchance, conform.

The term Philosophy of History is a formal and even a forbidding one. It conjures up for us those system makers and systems of the past, and of the present, too, who organized full scale philosophies of history and demanded that history shoulder arms and march to its commands: an Augustine who proved that history was the working out of the will of God with man, a Hegel with his mystical sense of history as the history of freedom culminating in the present, a Condorcet who saw all history as a serried panorama of progress, a Karl Marx with his iron laws of history as a record of the struggle for material ends, a John Fiske with his assurance that history was progressive evolution, a Henry Adams imposing an irrelevant law of thermodynamics on the reluctant stuff of history, a Benedetto Croce with his magisterial principle that all history is contemporary history and must be recaptured and realized by each historian for himself, an Arnold Toynbee with his theory of the rise and dispersion of civilizations.

As we contemplate these and many other philosophies of history we are forced to conclude that the effort to compress the incalculably vast, infinitely complex, and wantonly elusive stuff of history into any single framework, or to express it in any single formula, is doomed to futility. This conclusion in turn suggests not so much that men have failed to solve the enigma of history as that there is no solution and possibly no enigma. Who are we, after all, to impose our will upon history? Who are we to require that it embrace our theories, dance to our tunes, march to our commands? Certainly nothing in the record of historical philosophy encourages us to believe that we can ever find some meaning in history upon which all sound men will agree.

Indeed the very multiplicity of historical philosophies and the inability of the most profound historians to agree on the meaning of history suggest that the philosophies are dictated not by history itself, but by circumstances, or by the temperament and the training of the historical philosophers.

All of this is entirely natural. After all, philosophers and saints have been brooding over the relation of man to God for thousands of years without arriving at a common religion. Philosophers and statesmen have been working out political theories for over two thousand years without arriving at one on which any large portion of mankind voluntarily agrees. Philosophers and teachers have been considering the nature of education for centuries, but we have not yet arrived at any generally accepted philosophy of education. Why should we expect an authoritative philosophy of history when we still lack authoritative philosophies of religion, politics, or education?

If the deductive approach to the philosophy of history is unprofitable, let us turn to the inductive. G. M. Trevelyan has well said that philosophy is not something you take to history, it is something you carry away from history. If we cannot impose our philosophical patterns upon history, let us see if history can impose philosophical lessons upon us.

This is, to be sure, a manner of speech. There is no such thing as "history" in the abstract, something which works out lessons and proceeds to impose them upon her disciples. What we mean when we say that "history" imposes its lessons is that after prolonged study and profound consideration of some chapter of history, the historian, like the educator, or the jurisprudent, or the political philosopher, may draw some general conclusions about its meaning, its purposes, and its value. Such considerations will have no scientific validity; they will have only the authority which may attach itself to the character and the reputation of the historian. But that is true in every non-scientific domain. If, over the years and centuries, learned and sagacious scholars from many different societies arrive at some common generalizations, may we not be justified in according these some degree of respect?

So, at least, men have thought in the past. "The great errors of the age are very useful," wrote Voltaire. "One cannot remind oneself too often of crimes and disasters. These, no matter what people say, can be forestalled. The history of the tyrant Christiern can prevent a nation from giving absolute power to a tyrant, and the undoing of Charles XII at Pultawa will warn a generation not to plunge too deeply into the Ukraine without supplies." That is combining the serious and the frivolous with a vengeance, but it suggests how the liveliest mind of the eighteenth century turned to history, and wrote it, too. Certainly the American Founding Fathers thought the study of history profitable. All of them were immersed in history, especially in the history of the ancient world; almost all of them wrote history. They drew with confidence on the history of the past to justify independence, to guide them along the paths of federalism, to provide examples for their every experiment in politics and government, to illuminate the problem of the reconciliation of liberty and order. The debates in the Federal Convention of 1787, the debates in the ratifying conventions, *The Federalist* papers—these are one continuous historical commentary. And so, too, the private letters of John Adams, Madison, Jefferson, Hamilton, Washington—it was always history they turned to, for examples and illustrations and morals. Nor were the resources of history exhausted with the ratification of the Constitution. Washington drew upon history when he warned his fellow countrymen against the baleful influence of factions and parties; Jefferson called upon it when he denounced the Alien and Sedition Acts and celebrated the long record of freedom from governmental tyranny; Calhoun invoked it to vindicate States' Rights, and Webster, in that eloquent appeal for a Union one and inseparable, which still has the power to quicken our heart-beats. Lincoln reviewed the history of the nation in his First Inaugural Address to prove that "the nation came before the states," and he began his Gettysburg Address with a reminder of what had happened four score and seven years ago—. A hundred other examples flood into our minds; it is sufficient to recall one of the most fateful. Winston Churchill, an historian as well as a maker of history, tells us that when at Chequers he heard the news of the attack on Pearl Harbor, he knew that Britain was saved. "I had studied the American Civil War, fought out to the last desperate inch . . . I went to bed and slept the sleep of the saved."

We have quoted before what is probably the most familiar of all definitions of History: "philosophy teaching by examples." The phrase is Bolingbroke's, but Dionysius of Halicarnassus said the same thing two thousand years ago, and fifteen centuries later, Sir Walter Raleigh, who was an historian as well as an explorer, wrote that "the end and scope of all history" is "to teach us by examples of times past such wisdom as may guide our desires and actions." No definition is more hackneyed; perhaps none is more acceptable.

Very well, then; if history is philosophy teaching by examples, what does it teach?

Candor forces us to confess that it teaches pretty much what historians or, more commonly, those who are in power, want taught. All too often, over the centuries, history has been the camp-follower of victorious armies, the champion of successful parties, the apologist of dominant classes, the protagonist of established religions. Indeed, so widespread is the exploitation of history for personal, partisan, religious, class, or national purposes, that we cannot but have some sympathy with Napoleon's remark that "history is a lie agreed upon," or with Matthew Arnold's reference to "that huge Mississippi of falsehood called history," or speculate how applicable to history is Justice Holme's sardonic definition of Truth: "the majority vote of that nation that can lick all others." How sobering it is that in almost every major war both sides have invoked history with complete assurance that it will respond. Over the years history has been made to do service for almost every cause. The rich and the powerful on both sides of the Atlantic invoked the history of the French Revolution to damn all popular reforms and protect their privileges. Southern planters used the history of Greece and Rome to prove that slavery was a beneficent institution, and essential to a high civilization. Hitler prostituted history to prove the superiority of the Aryans over all other races. The Chinese Communists today rewrite history to prove that the white races have always exploited the yellow. Even in smaller matters politicians do not hesitate to summon up history to vindicate their arguments: that inflation always leads to ruin, or that centralization inevitably leads to tyranny, or that socialization destroys initiative, or that the majority have a peculiar proclivity for injustice.

If this were the whole story, we might well conclude that the study of history was at best an idle self-indulgence, and at worst corrupting; a number of critics have come to just that conclusion—Nietzsche and Verlaine among them. Happily it is not the whole story. History has other and more benevolent uses. It can, and does, provide mankind with memory. It does fire the imagination, broaden intellectual horizons, and deepen sympathies. It does summon up a great cloud of witnesses from the past to instruct and edify each new generation. It does encourage each generation to believe that it can build upon the past and perhaps progress into the future. And it does inculcate moral precepts.

What moral precepts? History provides perspective. It reminds us that time is indeed long and our own life fleeting; that for thousands of years each generation has thought that it was the end and the object of history; that men have known crises before, and wars, and turmoils, and triumph and tragedy, and have survived; that those issues and problems which loom so large on our horizons may not even be visible on the larger horizon of history; and that the cloud-capp'd towers, the gorgeous palaces, the solemn temples, which to us seem the very wonders of the world, may dissolve and leave not a rack behind.

Because history gives us a larger perspective, it moderates our instinctive and pervasive parochialism, a parochialism of both time and space, a parochialism which is moral as well as social or political. It teaches us that the world is large, miscellaneous, and haphazard, not subject to our fiat or to our desires. It tells us that one people and then another, one nation and then another, one civilization and then another has moved to the center of the historical stage, and claimed for itself the principal role, and then moved into the shadows. It admonishes us that our habits and interests, our standards and values, have no cosmic validity; that we cannot impose our will upon history, or bestride history like some Colossus. It teaches therefore modesty and humility.

Along with these precepts history enjoins patience—patience with the long struggle of men to conquer Nature, to organize government and society, to cope with the thousand problems that glare and glower upon them ceaselessly through time. It teaches patience with the errors of men, the mischief of their enterprises, the failures of their institutions, the frustrations of their hopes and ambitions. It teaches patience too with our own contemporaries, patience with those who, in the words of Jefferson describing the French Revolution, "seek through blood and slaughter their long-lost liberties"; patience with those who are just now emerging out of centuries of darkness and deprivation and are trying to catch up, in one convulsive leap, with the peoples of the western world; patience with those who do not accept or adopt our ways of thinking or adopt our institutions; patience with experiments that seem misguided and even pernicious. It counsels us to be patient with the unfathomable processes of history, the unexpected, the unforeseen, the unfamiliar; with change that never comes the way we want it to come; with problems that are never solved the way we would solve them, or that are simply transformed into new problems equally insoluble. It teaches us patience with all of this, but impatience with all those simplifications which do violence to the mysterious complexity, the subtlety, the richness and density and intricacy of the historical process.

History teaches tolerance—tolerance with different faiths, different loyalties, different cultures, different ideas and ideals. It instructs us that over the centuries there have been so many of these, so many faiths, so many cultures, so many nations, so many parties, so many philosophies, that each people has been guilty of supposing, "Lo we are the people and all wisdom dies with us"; that each sect, each party, has indulged in the vanity of believing that it, somehow, represented the larger purposes of history and the will of God. It teaches tolerance of alien peoples and opposing interests, and of ideas which, in the words of Justice Holmes, we think "loathsome and fraught with death." It teaches, therefore, the necessity of freedom—freedom for inquiry, freedom for heterodoxy and dissent—for it makes clear that freedom is the only method mankind has thus far found for avoiding error and discovering truth.

History assures us that man is neither the creature of iron laws over which he has no control nor the victim of chance and fortuity. Man need not sink beneath some secular determinism, nor need he acquiesce in the notion that day after day the wind of history bloweth where it listeth, and that he is the sport of vagrant historical winds. For history tells us that if men are not masters of their fate, neither are they the victims of fate. It reminds us, by a thousand stirring examples, that the individual counts, that character counts. It makes clear that it was the genius of Mohammed that revitalized the Arab world, that it was the moral power of the Maid of Orleans which united the French against the English; that the iron will of Cromwell was essential to the triumph of the Puritan cause; that it was Washington who made possible the American victory in the Revolutionary War, that Mahatma Gandhi was the driving force behind Indian independence and nationhood, and that without Winston Churchill's eloquence and resolution, England might have gone under before help could have arrived from across the sea.

And does not history tell us, too, that it is not only the character of the individual but of a whole people that counts? "What kind of a people do they think we are?" cried Churchill at a famous moment in history, and may we not say that it was because Hitler and his supporters were ignorant and contemptuous of history that they failed so fatefully to understand what kind of people the British were. The character of a people counts, and makes a difference—in the long nightmare struggle of the Dutch against their Spanish overlords, in the bulldog tenacity of the British against the Napoleonic imperium, in the passionate patriotism and courage of the Swiss, in the courage, the prudence, the industry, the wisdom of the Norwegians in surviving through Nazi tyranny and rebuilding their shattered nation after liberation.

And history reminds us, too, that character is to be read not only in manifestations of courage and power, but in things of the mind and the spirit as well. We do not turn to the histories of ancient Athens, of Renaissance Florence and Siena, of Elizabethan England or colonial Virginia or nineteenth century Denmark because they recount great deeds of courage or mighty strokes of power, but because they provide us with refreshment of the mind and the spirit. History admonishes us that the tests of happiness, of greatness, and of power are not everywhere or always the same, and that in the long run what we turn to are not the triumphs of wealth and of might but of the mind and the spirit of man.

It is not given us to know the causes of things, but the search for causes is itself an affluent enterprise, one which enlarges the mind and quickens the sympathies of all who engage in it. No laws of history command authority, but the study of those manifold forces which ceaselessly play upon history deepens our understanding and brings magnanimity to our judgment. No philosophy encompasses or explains the trackless course of history, but to those who study it with sympathy and understanding and imagination history teaches philosophy. *Esto perpetuo.*

Bibliography

Acton, Lord. *Essays on Freedom and Power,* ed. by Gertrude Himmelfarb. Boston: Beacon Press, 1948.

Ausubel, Herman. *Historians and Their Craft: A Study of the Presidential Addresses to the American Historical Association, 1884–1945.* New York: Columbia University Press, 1952.

————, et al. *Some Modern Historians of Britain, Essays in Honor of R. L. Schuyler.* New York: Holt, Rinehart & Winston, Inc., 1951.

Barraclough, Geoffrey. *History in a Changing World.* New York: Oxford University Press, 1955.

Barzun, Jacques and Graff, Henry A. *The Modern Researcher.* New York: Harcourt, Brace & World, Inc., 1957.

Bassett, John Spencer. *The Middle Group of American Historians.* New York: The Macmillan Company, 1917.

Beard, Charles A. *The Economic Basis of Politics.* New York: Random House, Inc., 1957.

Becker, Carl. *Everyman His Own Historian.* New York: Appleton-Century-Crofts, 1935.

Berlin, Isaiah. *Historical Inevitability.* New York: Oxford University Press, 1954.

Bloch, Marc. *The Historian's Craft.* New York: Alfred A. Knopf, Inc., 1953.

Bowen, Catherine Drinker. *Adventures of a Biographer.* Boston: Atlantic-Little, Brown, 1959.

Bury, J. B. *The Ancient Greek Historians.* New York: The Macmillan Company, 1909.

————. *The Idea of Progress.* New York: The Macmillan Company, 1932.

Butterfield, Herbert. *The Englishman and His History.* Cambridge: Cambridge University Press, 1944.

———. *History and Human Relations.* London: Collins, 1951.

———. *Man on His Past: The Study of the History of Historical Scholarship.* Cambridge: Cambridge University Press, 1954.

Carr, Edward Hallett. *What Is History?* New York: Alfred A. Knopf, Inc., 1962.

Cassirer, Ernst. *The Philosophy of the Enlightenment.* Boston: Beacon Press, 1951.

Cheyney, Edward P. *Law in History and Other Essays.* New York: Alfred A. Knopf, Inc., 1927.

Collingwood, R. G. *The Idea of History.* Oxford: Clarendon Press, 1946.

Dilthey, Wilhelm. *Pattern and Meaning in History.* New York: Harper & Row, Publishers, 1961.

Dunning, William A. *Truth in History and Other Essays,* intro. by J. G. DeRoulhac Hamilton. New York: Columbia University Press, 1937.

Flint, Robert. *History of the Philosophy of History.* Edinburgh and London: William Blackwood and Sons, 1893.

Gardiner, Patrick, ed. *Theories of History: Readings from Classical and Contemporary Sources.* New York: Free Press of Glencoe, Inc., 1959.

Geyl, Pieter. *Debates with Historians.* Cleveland: The World Publishing Co., 1958.

———. *Encounters in History.* New York: Meridian Books, Inc., 1961.

Gooch, G. P. *History and Historians in the Nineteenth Century,* 2nd ed. New York: David McKay Co., Inc., 1952.

Gottschalk, Louis. *Generalization in the Writing of History.* Chicago: The University of Chicago Press, 1963.

———. *Understanding History.* New York: Alfred A. Knopf, Inc., 1950.

Harrison, Frederic. *The Meaning of History.* New York: The Macmillan Company, 1908.

Hexter, J. H. *Reappraisals in History.* Evanston, Ill.: Northwestern University Press, 1961.

Hughes, H. Stuart. *History as Art and as Science.* New York: Harper & Row, Publishers, 1964.

Hutchinson, William T., ed. *The Marcus W. Jernegan Essays in American Historiography.* Chicago: University of Chicago Press, 1937.

Kent, Sherman. *Writing History.* New York: Appleton-Century-Crofts, 1941.

Kichan, Lionel. *Action on History.* London: Deutsch, 1954.

Klibansky, Raymond and Paton, H. J., eds. *Philosophy and History.* New York, Evanston, and London: Harper & Row, Publishers, 1963.

Knowles, David. *The Historian and Character.* Cambridge: Cambridge University Press, 1963.

Kraus, Michael. *A History of American History.* New York: Farrar and Rinehart, 1937.

Laistner, M. L. W. *The Greater Roman Historians.* Berkeley: University of California Press, 1947.

Leisy, Ernest E. *The American Historical Novel.* Norman, Okla.: University of Oklahoma Press, 1950.

Levin, David. *History as Romantic Art: Bancroft, Prescott, Motley, and Parkman.* Stanford, Calif.: Stanford University Press, 1959.

Lovejoy, Arthur O. *Essays in the History of Ideas.* Baltimore: Johns Hopkins Press, 1948.

Malin, James. *The Contriving Brain and the Skillful Hand in the United States: Something About History and the Philosophy of History.* Lawrence, Kan.: University of Kansas Press, 1955.

————. *Essays on Historiography.* Lawrence, Kan.: University of Kansas Press, 1946.

————. *On the Nature of History: Essays about History and Dissidence.* Lawrence, Kan.: University of Kansas Press, 1954.

Meyerhoff, Hans. *The Philosophy of History in Our Time: An Anthology Selected and Edited by Hans Meyerhoff.* Garden City, N. Y.: Doubleday & Company, Inc., 1959.

Morison, Samuel Eliot. *Vistas of History.* New York: Alfred A. Knopf, Inc., 1964.

Muller, Herbert J. *The Uses of the Past.* New York: Columbia University Press, 1952.

Namier, L. B. *Avenues of History.* London: Hamish Hamilton, 1952.

Neff, Emery. *The Poetry of History.* New York: Columbia University Press, 1947.

Nevins, Allan. *The Gateway to History.* Garden City, N. Y.: Doubleday & Company, Inc., 1962.

————, "Not Capulets, Not Montagus," *American Historical Review,* LXV (1960), 253–271.

Niebuhr, Reinhold. *The Irony of American History.* New York: Charles Scribner's Sons, 1952.

Nietzsche, Frederick. *The Use and Abuse of History.* New York: Liberal Arts Press, 1949.

Pares, Richard. *The Historian's Business and Other Essays,* ed. by R. A. and Elisabeth Humphreys. New York: Oxford University Press, 1961.

Popper, Karl. *The Poverty of Historicism.* Boston: Beacon Press, 1957.

Renier, Gustaf J. *History, Its Purpose and Method*. Boston: Beacon Press, 1950.

Rowse, A. L. *The Use of History*. New York: The Macmillan Co., 1947.

Salmon, Lucy M. *Why Is History Rewritten?* intro. by Edward P. Cheney. New York: Oxford University Press, 1929.

Schevill, Ferdinand. *Six Historians*. Chicago: University of Chicago Press, 1956.

Smith, Page. *The Historian and History*. New York: Alfred A. Knopf, Inc., 1964.

Stern, Fritz, ed. *Varieties of History*. New York: Meridian Books, Inc., 1956.

Strayer, Joseph R., ed. *The Interpretation of History*. Princeton, N. J.: Princeton University Press, 1943.

Strout, Cushing. *The Pragmatic Revolt in American History: Carl Becker and Charles Beard*. New Haven, Conn.: Yale University Press, 1958.

Teggart, Frederick J. *The Processes of History*. New Haven, Conn.: Yale University Press, 1918.

———. *Prolegomena to History: The Relation of History to Literature, Philosophy, and Science*. Berkeley: University of California Press, 1916.

———. *Theory and Processes of History*. Berkeley: University of California Press, 1941.

Thompson, J. W. *A History of Historical Writing*. New York: The Macmillan Company, 1942. 2 vols.

Trevelyan, George Macaulay. *Clio, A Muse and Other Essays*. London: Longmans, Green, 1913. 2nd ed., 1930.

———. *An Autobiography and Other Essays*. London: 1949.

Wedgwood, C. V. *The Sense of the Past*. New York: Columbia University Press, 1957.

———. *Truth and Opinion*. London: Collins; New York: The Macmillan Company, 1960.

Weiss, Paul. *History, Written and Lived*. Carbondale, Ill.: Southern Illinois University Press, 1962.

Wish, Harvey. *The American Historian*. New York: Oxford University Press, 1960.

———, ed. *American Historians, A Selection*. New York: Oxford University Press, 1962.

Suggested Methods for Teachers

chapter six

Raymond H. Muessig
Vincent R. Rogers

> It is my earnest hope that pondering upon the past may give guidance in days to come, enable a new generation to repair some of the errors of former years and thus govern, in accordance with the needs and glory of man, the awful unfolding scene of the future.
>
> SIR WINSTON CHURCHILL

Man is now and probably always has been immensely curious about his past. From almost the dawn of civilization he has mulled over relics, scribblings, paintings, buildings, tombs, letters, documents, and diaries in an effort to know what happened before him; modern man spends vast amounts of money on antiques and other vestiges of the past; he often plans vacation trips around national shrines and historic sites, and reverently tells his children the legends and stories he has been told about the great men of the past. Children and youth, too, appear to share in this curiosity. Study after study indicates that "people who lived long ago," "pioneers," "explorers," "olden times," and other similar topics are among those most mentioned in investigations of young peoples' interests—even though "history" as a school subject is not often rated very high.

It seems that it is our task as teachers to harness this interest, to build and elaborate upon it in such a way that the study of the past begins to take on new meaning, value, and excitement for our students.

Given the space limitations of this chapter, we cannot suggest a new history curriculum, program, theory, or perspective; none of the ideas that follow are guarantees of success and salvation. We can, however, attempt to illustrate a number of Professor Commager's most compelling ideas through situations and topics often dealt with by most teachers with the hope that at least some of our ideas may be adopted or adapted for classroom use.

1. Continuous and Unrelenting Change Has Been a Universal Condition of Human Society Throughout Both Remembered and Recorded Time.

There is nothing permanent except change, Heraclitus once observed. Every literate, sensitive human being who studies his extended and more immediate heritage and who looks at the images and listens to the sounds that surround him daily is impressed again and again with the omnipresence of change. A person can see the face of change in weather-worn, moss-covered buildings and monuments that tell a story of past events. He can hear the recorded voice of a great statesman who no longer walks the halls of a governmental edifice in which history has been and is being made. He can savor the taste of foods now readily available to him which were once unknown to mankind. And he can feel the smooth texture of the wooden handle on a tool used laboriously for a purpose which is now non-existent.

We believe that our children and youth can gain deeper understandings of the nature and implications of aspects of change through their study of carefully selected and creatively taught elements of history. In this brief section we have illustrated procedures which might help teachers to illuminate several facets of the idea of change as seen through an historical perspective. Teachers will doubtless think of other properties and ramifications of change as well as alternative activities and materials which could be employed.

At various grade levels, teachers could help their charges look at changes that have taken place during the life of an individual, prominent or not, about whom data can be uncovered in countless sources that have historical overtones. With junior and senior high school students, for example, the teacher might draw upon some of the abundant materials that reveal changes in the life of Abraham Lincoln. Using a resource such as *The Life and Writings of Abraham Lincoln*,[1] edited by Philip

---

[1] New York: Modern Library, Inc., 1940.

Van Doren Stern, the teacher might preface his reading aloud of selected passages from Lincoln's speeches by sharing with his class one of the introductory comments to this book which were penned by Allan Nevins:

> Lincoln slowly developed great inner reservoirs of strength, which enabled him to meet each new demand, each fresh crisis of his life, not merely adequately but with inspiration. The awakened opponent of slavery-expansion after the Kansas-Nebraska Bill was clearly greater than the author of the Peoria speech; and the Lincoln of the Gettysburg Address and the Second Inaugural was greater—far greater—than the Lincoln whose silk hat Douglas held as he first took the oath of office. We can trace this development in his speeches and letters, and we can catch glimpses there of the deep springs which fed his inner reservoirs of power.[2]

Portions of Lincoln's speeches could be read aloud to the class by the teacher or played from available recordings such as those made by Raymond Massey from Lincoln's first public address of March 9, 1832; his speech given at Peoria in reply to Senator Douglas on October 16, 1854; his letter to Joshua F. Speed, dated August 24, 1855; his speech delivered in Springfield on June 16, 1858, at the Republican State Convention; his Cooper Union address given on February 27, 1860; his farewell address at Springfield, February 11, 1861; his First Inaugural Address on March 4, 1861; his letter to Horace Greeley on August 22, 1862; his August 26, 1863, letter to James C. Conkling; his Gettysburg Address voiced on November 19, 1863; and his last public address, April 11, 1865.

Students should be invited to identify differences in these writings in tone, impact, and sophistication, and to discuss some of the changes in Lincoln the man and Lincoln the statesman which they reveal.

In a similar vein, secondary school students could discuss changes in the life of Lincoln as revealed dramatically in the play, *Abe Lincoln in Illinois*, by Robert E. Sherwood.[3] Or, teachers at the intermediate, junior high, and senior high school levels could display or project on an opaque projector a series of cartoons which depict changes in the life of a given political figure. Albert Shaw's *A Cartoon History of Roosevelt's Career*[4] and Jay N. Darling's *As Ding Saw Hoover*[5] are examples of sources which could be used.

---

[2] *Ibid.*, p. xix.

[3] In John Gassner (ed.), *Best Plays of the Modern American Theatre: Second Series* (New York: Crown Publishers, Inc., 1947).

[4] New York: The Review of Reviews Company, Publishers, 1910.

[5] Ames, Iowa: Iowa State University Press, 1954.

One of the most telling portraits of change in a particular individual is Betty Fladeland's thorough study, *James Gillespie Birney: Slaveholder to Abolitionist.*[6] Senior high school students could be encouraged to discuss and helped to comprehend the complete metamorphosis which took place in Birney's life. As a boy, Birney had his own slave. When he was married, he and his bride received several household slaves as gifts from their parents. By 1821 Birney had purchased nineteen Negroes, thus bringing the total of the slaves he owned to forty-three. Slavery was a confusing issue to Birney at times in his earlier years, but he had accepted it in practice in a benevolent fashion if not in principle. It is significant for students to discover, therefore, that he changed to the extent that he freed his own slaves, became an active abolitionist, and ran as a presidential candidate for the Liberty party because of his altered convictions. It is especially telling that as a founder of a local church in 1846 he wrote an article of faith expressing a belief in the equality of man.

Children and youth at all instructional levels could explore as well evidence of change in a particular locale over an extended period of time. It is quite easy, for instance, for the enterprising teacher (or his pupils) to collect photographs and written materials concerned with the same place which span a number of years and tell a story of change. Long-time residents of a community may be willing to loan their pictures or other materials to students, or, better yet, to bring them to a class session to buttress and illustrate their personal narratives. Senior citizens who cannot come to the school could be contacted by small groups of pupils and their tape-recorded stories of community changes brought to the classroom for an entire class to hear and discuss. Local businesses which have occupied the same spot for many years may have a collection of pictures, posters, advertisements, and the like, which portray transformations in their facilities. Some newspapers will make available to school classes photographs or copies of past newspapers which dramatize in visual and written form transitions in local sites familiar to students; or they will welcome a class or smaller committee of pupils to their plants where these materials can be examined. Perhaps even the school district central office itself could be tapped as a resource for materials which describe modifications in programs and plants which could be analyzed. Older high schools may have substantial data in their files, including copies of former yearbooks, which could be used for research and discussion. Students might become involved to the extent that they would write a brief history of changes in their school district in general or their own school in particular.

---

[6] Ithaca: Cornell University Press, 1955.

Children in elementary schools could be introduced to changes in a given area through a book such as Janice Holland's *They Built a City,*[7] which describes the birth and growth of our Capitol city. Upper elementary, junior, and senior high school teachers might turn to a source like Josef and Dorothy Berger's compelling *Diary of America* to confront their students with the idea of change as evidenced in transformations that have taken place in certain areas. Below are passages from three diaries which describe New York. The first account was written by Jasper Danckaerts in 1679, when New York had a population of around 3,500. The second group of excerpts, from the pen of Philip Hone, a wealthy New York businessman, were written in 1832 and 1836. Simone de Beauvoir, the French writer, describes her feeling about New York during a visit in 1947 in the third group of excerpts.

This island (Manhattan) is about seven hours' distance in length, but it is not a full hour broad. The sides are indented with bays, coves and creeks. It is almost entirely taken up, that is the land is held by private owners, but not half of it is cultivated. Much of it is good wood land. The west end on which the city lies, is entirely cleared for more than an hour's distance, though that is the poorest ground; the best being on the east and north side.

There are many brooks of fresh water running through it, pleasant and proper for man and beast to drink, as well as agreeable to behold, affording cool and pleasant resting places, but especially suitable places for the construction of mills.

The Camden & Amboy Railroad was opened on Monday on the whole line, and passengers who left New York in the steamboat for Amboy at half past six were in Philadelphia about two. This is expected to be the best joint stock property in the United States.

. . . .

There arrived at this port, during the month of May, 15,825 passengers. All Europe is coming across the ocean; all that part at least who cannot make a living at home; and what shall we do with them? They increase our taxes, eat our bread, and encumber our streets, and not one in twenty is competent to keep himself.

We were just waiting our turn: there is an airplane landing every minute at La Guardia Airport. . . . We followed the line of a river, crossed over an iron bridge, and suddenly my neighbor said, "This is Broadway." Then, at a glance I saw it—great luminous streets in which hundreds and hundreds of cars were moving, stopping and starting again with such discipline that they appeared to be controlled by some magnetic providence from the skies above.

[7] New York: Charles Scribner's Sons, 1953, pp. not numbered.

We took a long time finding a place to park the car.

D. P. had booked a room for me in a huge hotel at the corner of Forty-fourth Street and Eighth Avenue.[8]

In addition to assisting children and youth to look into changes in persons and places, teachers might also aid their classes to investigate alterations in "things"—that is, technological and scientific modifications clarified by a focused study of specific inventions, techniques, processes, and so on. An entire class could trace the development of a single object or procedure; smaller committees could center their attention upon specific subjects; or each pupil might select his own area of exploration. For example, time indicators and timekeepers could be researched at various instructional levels. Through a trip to a local museum, a resource person, books picturing and discussing the history of time, realia brought into the classroom, and models constructed to demonstrate the more simple devices used throughout the ages, pupils could familiarize themselves with the sundial, the clepsydra, the sand glass, the notched candle, the graduated lamp, the clock, the pocket watch, the wristwatch, and such later innovations as the self-winding watch and the battery-powered watch. The teacher or one of his students might like to write for a free publication such as the Bulova Time Center's interestingly written and well illustrated booklet *You and Time: The Fascinating Story of Timekeeping* [9] as a tailor-made resource. Better still, both teacher and student might turn to Thelma and Corydon Bell's *The Riddle of Time* for a fascinating, scholarly treatment of the subject.[10]

Or, the teacher might bring into class a collection of early American household objects such as a footwarmer, a lantern, a candle holder, a porringer, a mousetrap, a door knocker, a mortar and pestle, a fireplace bellows, a boot scraper, a live coal carrier, etc, and display them without any identification. Students could be asked to identify the object; to trace its origin; to explain its design, construction, use, and any interesting points or problems associated with that use; and to follow changes made in the object or the discontinuation of its use. In some instances, pupils would find substantial alterations in the object, and in other cases they might be surprised to see how little change has been made in it.

The history of the airplane could also be used by the teacher as an illustration of change in one of man's inventions and the transformations in his way of life wrought by technological innovation. No readily available resource enriches, vivifies, and personifies the early story of advances

---

[8] Josef and Dorothy Berger (eds.), *Diary of America* (New York: Simon and Schuster, Inc., 1957), pp. 32, 201–205, 605.

[9] Bulova Watch Company, Inc. (Bulova Park, Flushing 70, New York, 1957).

[10] New York: The Viking Press, 1963.

in the field of aviation more than *The Papers of Wilbur and Orville Wright,* which Marvin W. McFarland has edited. This excellent primary source permits the reader to trace the work of the Wright brothers from dream to reality. The teacher, for example, might read to his students in the upper elementary or secondary grades this touching portion of a letter written by Wilbur Wright to Octave Chanute on May 13, 1900:

> For some years I have been afflicted with the belief that flight is possible to man. My disease has increased in severity and I feel that it will soon cost me an increased amount of money if not my life. . . .[11]

This excerpt from Orville Wright's deposition of January 13, 1920, in *Regina C. Montgomery* et al. vs. *the United States,* in response to the question of the defendant's counsel is also revealing and appealing:

> Our first interest began when we were children. Father brought home to us a small toy actuated by a rubber spring which would lift itself into the air. We built a number of copies of this toy, which flew successfully. By "we" I refer to my brother Wilbur and myself. But when we undertook to build the toy on a much larger scale it failed to work so well. The reason for this was not understood by us at the time, so we finally abandoned the experiments. In 1896 we read in the daily papers, or in some of the magazines, of the experiments of Otto Lilienthal, who was making some gliding flights from the top of a small hill in Germany. His death a few months later while making a glide off the hill increased our interest in the subject, and we began looking for books pertaining to flight. We found a work written by Professor Marey on animal mechanism which treated of the bird mechanism as applied to flight, but other than this, so far as I can remember, we found little.
>
> In the spring of the year 1899 our interest in the subject was again aroused through the reading of a book on ornithology. We could not understand that there was anything about a bird that would enable it to fly that could not be built on a larger scale and used by man. . . .[12]

The teacher might also read the triumphant, though frugal and laconic, telegram sent by Orville Wright to Bishop Milton Wright from Kitty Hawk on December 17, 1903:

> Success four flights Thursday morning all against twenty-one mile wind started from level with engine power alone average speed through air thirty-one miles longest 57 seconds inform press home Christmas.[13]

---

[11] From *The Papers of Wilbur and Orville Wright,* I (1899–1905), 15, Marvin W. McFarland (ed.). Copyright 1953 by McGraw-Hill Book Company. Used by permission of McGraw-Hill Book Company.

[12] *Ibid.,* p. 3.

[13] *Ibid.,* p. 397.

In the event that girls in the class might feel less interested in the study of inventions such as the airplane, the teacher might like to add changes in diet, foods, and food processing endeavors over the years. Girls, for example, might investigate changes that have occurred in the preservation of foods and resulting alterations in life-ways facilitated by these improvements. They could trace the invention of canning from Napoleon's desire for foods that could be preserved for his soldiers to the work of Peter Durand in England with "cans," the scientific discoveries of Louis Pasteur, the development of a unique canning jar perfected by John L. Mason, Alexander Kerr's lid with a sealing gasket, and so on. By chatting with their grandmothers they would discover that women spent endless hours in the kitchen preparing and preserving foods which may be given to other pursuits today due to the availability of commercially canned and frozen foods.

Children and youth from the intermediate through the senior high school levels could also be introduced to changes in words, modes of expression, forms of communication, and ideas from age to age and culture to culture.

Below are just a few words which have an interesting origin or heritage and which should give teachers an idea of countless other words (suited to the educational level of students in a given class, of course) which could be used for classroom study:

paper	alphabet	America	greenhorn
sandwich	bugle	colonel	school
August	England	hamburger	diesel
revolver	democracy	maverick	tycoon
barbarian	camp	ostracize	algebra

At various conceptual stages, children and youth might deal as well with figures in history who effected changes or served as agents for change in many fields of endeavor. Elementary teachers, for example, could read to youngsters or have them read selected simplified biographies of well-known personages such as scientists—like Leeuwenhoek, Pasteur, and Reed, treated so ably by Paul de Kruif in *Microbe Hunters* [14] —and numerous others.

Secondary students might be challenged to grapple briefly with the "great man theory" through a study and discussion of quotations from historians and writers such as Emerson who wrote that "there is properly no History, only Biography" and that "an institution is the lengthened

---

[14] New York: Pocket Books, Inc., 1926.

shadow of one man . . . and all history resolves itself very easily into the biography of a few stout and earnest persons." Older students might also read about and discuss the influence of writer-reformers like Charles Dickens, Harriet Beecher Stowe, Susan B. Anthony, Jane Addams, and Lincoln Steffens.

There are many ways, too, of aiding students to look at facets of social and legislative change. Three representative sources which might be employed in various ways at the intermediate and junior high school levels for this purpose are Genevieve Foster's *Birthdays of Freedom: From the Fall of Rome to July 4, 1776*,[15] Richard B. Morris' *The First Book of the Constitution*,[16] and Henry Steele Commager's *The Great Proclamation*.[17]

Foster's book traces legal developments such as Charlemagne's uniform laws, Anglo-Saxon laws, the Magna Carta, and so on. *The First Book of the Constitution* moves through the state constitutions, the Articles of Confederation, the conventions in Annapolis and Philadelphia, the New Jersey Plan and the Virginia Plan, the Great Compromise, the great fight for ratification, the debates in Virginia and New York, the adoption of the Constitution, the Bill of Rights, and the Amendments. Commager's *The Great Proclamation* handles events which led up to the Emancipation Proclamation and which culminated in the Thirteenth Amendment to the Constitution.

Another very important dimension of change which could be interpreted meaningfully in our schools is the fundamental historical observation that some things seem to be more permanent than others, although the reasons for this permanence are not always apparent or consistent. While change is always taking place, it does not occur at a uniform rate from generation to generation and from locale to locale. The persistence of a particular idea, belief, value, practice, process, institution, etc., is not a guarantee of its merit or effectiveness. Neither is change—in and of itself—synonymous with "progress."

One possible way for the teacher to give his students some perception of permanence is for him to display copies of various written materials (posters, newspapers, magazines, books, letters, diaries, speeches, documents, etc.), and to ask his students to discuss the length of time which a given work seems to have influenced a significant number of people and the intensity of this influence. The following are just a few items— arranged purposely in a random fashion—which might be shown to class members for this purpose:

---

[15] New York: Charles Scribner's Sons, 1957, Book 2.

[16] New York: Franklin Watts, Inc., 1958.

[17] Indianapolis: The Bobbs-Merrill Co., Inc., 1960.

A clipping from a daily newspaper advertising a one-day sale at a local department store.

A copy of the Old Testament.

A copy of the United Nations Charter.

A magazine article reporting an interview with an important figure in government concerning his views on an issue currently before the public.

A reprint of a speech delivered by the losing candidate in a Presidential campaign.

A copy of the Mayflower Compact.

A copy of a poster promoting the sale of war bonds.

A copy of the Bill of Rights.

A copy of General McAuliffe's "Merry Christmas" message to the members of the 101st Airborne Division on Christmas Eve of 1944.[18]

Obviously, there will not be uniform agreement on the enduring value and impact of some of the items which the teacher may display while employing this approach. But students will certainly be able to see that there can be wide differences in the degree of permanence which written and other materials may enjoy.

Variations in the rate of change from time to time and place to place can be made evident to elementary and secondary students through a variety of procedures. One possibility is for the teacher to read to the class from Genevieve Foster's *George Washington's World,* a unique and helpful approach to change in a chronological context. Using Washington's life as the center of focus, Foster treats numerous events (the invention of the steam engine, Cook's discovery of Australia, the birth of Napoleon, the settling of California, etc.) taking place at the same time in different parts of the world (Prussia, England, France, Italy, Spain, Turkey, Poland, Russia, China, Japan, etc.). This excerpt is representative of the format Foster has developed:

In those years England, the small island kingdom off the coast of Europe, had been putting down strong roots of what was to become a great world empire. But Japan, the similarly small island off the coast of

---

[18] By arrangement with the American Heritage Foundation, which sponsored the Freedom Train, the *Chicago Tribune* has published *Forty Documents of the Freedom Train,* a folder which contains reproductions of McAuliffe's message, the United Nations Charter, the Mayflower Compact, the Bill of Rights, Thomas Paine's "Common Sense," the original manuscript of the "Star Spangled Banner," etc. This interesting collection may be secured from the *Chicago Tribune,* Tribune Tower, Chicago 11, Illinois.

Asia, had been wrapped up in itself as tight as a cocoon, and was to find, many years later when she wished to extend into a great empire, that the days of exploration were over and that there were no lands to conquer not already claimed by civilized nations.[19]

A discussion of Foster's book [20] should quickly bring out among class members an awareness of differential rates of change within and among various societies, nations, and continents. With high school students, the teacher might launch a study of variegated patterns of change in a number of cultures. Committees of from three to five young people could be formed and each of the groups assigned a different century to investigate. Each committee might start with a source such as William L. Langer's *An Encyclopedia of World History* [21] as a means of identifying some changes taking place all over the world during the specified century and would then turn to other research materials. Using the same scale, every group of students would next prepare a timeline for its century— listing some significant, interesting, perhaps representative changes that took place. Students should catch some revealing comparisons in the rate of change from culture to culture and century to century. For example, they might contrast in some depth Moslem (especially in places such as Toledo and Cordova) and Christian societies during the eighth through the twelfth centuries. Or they could compare the so-called Dark Ages in medieval Europe with the centuries before Mohammed (termed Djahiliya, or roughly, the Age of Ignorance or Illiteracy) in the areas which embraced the religion of Islam.

In a similar vein, junior and senior high school students studying the history of the United States might explore variations in the rate of change from decade to decade and section to section of America. They could use a source such as the *Encyclopedia of American History*,[22] edited by Richard B. Morris, as a point of embarkation. After consulting the *Encyclopedia of American History* and many other references, students might try to create a large, simple poster or mural which would be a "profile of change" and which would graphically portray accelerations, peaks, plateaus, decelerations, and valleys of change over the years in different parts of the country. Various written materials discussing the very rapid changes that have taken place in the United States in the past few decades could also be read aloud and discussed.

---

[19] Genevieve Foster, *George Washington's World* (New York: Charles Scribner's Sons, 1941).

[20] Foster has written a second book employing a similar technique: *Abraham Lincoln's World* (New York: Charles Scribner's Sons, 1944).

[21] Boston: Houghton Mifflin Company, 1952.

[22] Rev. ed.; New York: Harper & Row, Publishers, 1961.

Finally, still another dimension of change might be approached through an historical frame of reference. Senior high school students might be given a glimpse of the inevitability of change and its tragedy on the one hand and challenge on the other. The teacher might invite students to write essays centered around a quotation such as the following and then to share their thinking with their classmates:

> . . . The process is endless. For no sooner is one ideal realized than it suggests a new and higher ideal—and so on forever. Never can man rest. Never can he look upon the world and say that it is good. Since the quest for perfection and truth is endless, its pursuit is both tragic and heroic . . . .[23]

2. History Makes Man Aware of the Possible Rather Than the Probable, Allowing Him to Choose Among Rational Alternatives Concerning the Time in Which He Lives. History Offers No Immutable Laws, Givens, or Inevitables, However, Upon Which to Base Such Decisions.

> . . . What an individual can do on a given occasion . . . is indeed circumscribed, but it is not predetermined. And, since everything in history arises from the interaction of human individuals, few of whom foresee what others will do in response to what they do, much less the whole pattern of their interaction, neither is the source of history predetermined. Both progress and retrogression are possible. Should history have any "meaning," it would be this: nothing happens in history except as the outcome, usually unforeseen, of free choices by individual men. If history is the slaughter-bench at which the human race is victimized, it is because of what some or all men have done, and not because of ineluctable material necessity or the cunning of the World Spirit.[24]

Comte, Hegel, Marx, Engles, Toynbee and others as well, dreamed about a vast historical pattern or plan that would explain the past and indicate directions for the future. While all made contributions to historical literature, most objective historians remain unconvinced that such patterns do, in fact, exist. Mankind seems always to be in a position where new and fateful decisions must be made; decisions that, if illuminated by the past, are certainly not dictated by it. As Crane Brinton put it, people have always felt they were "facing the horrible 'either-or'—and found that somehow there were almost infinite possi-

---

[23] Agnes E. Meyer, *Education for a New Morality* (New York: The Macmillan Company, 1957), p. 89.

[24] Alan and Barbara Donagan, *Philosophy of History* (New York: The Macmillan Company, 1965), pp. 21–22.

bilities in between." [25] No matter how well we "know" history, we still find ourselves torn between crucial, complex alternatives in crisis after crisis.

This is not to say, of course, that man does not profit from the lessons of the past, that he cannot learn from history. The problem is (in Louis Gottschalk's words) that he can be "*counted* upon neither to do so or *not* to do so." [26]

In this sense, all historical decisions were at one time open questions, just as today's decisions (which will become tomorrow's history) are similarly open. Contemporary man may only evaluate the choices made in the past and attempt to find meaningful alternatives for today's decisions, recognizing (as Shakespeare did in Julius Caesar) that if he chooses poorly, "The fault, dear Brutus, is not in our stars, / But in ourselves . . ."

The notion that individuals living through what we have come to view as momentous and exciting periods in history were still individuals, able for the most part to choose among alternative courses of action and *not* predestined for a given fate, might well be explored through studies of the westward movement. For example, most children in today's intermediate grades have the impression that selling a house or farm, packing up, and "going west" was the natural thing to do in pioneer days. They imagine that family after family did so, scarcely giving the matter a second thought. Moving west was, of course, a far more complicated matter. Many factors had to be considered, and the decision to pull up stakes was seldom an easy one to make.

During their study of the westward movement, then, a group of fifth graders might be told to imagine that they are living on a rocky, rather unproductive New England farm during the year 1867. One evening an older brother bursts into the kitchen with this poster clutched in his hand.

FARMS AND HOMES IN KANSAS
EMIGRANTS
Look to Your
INTEREST
FARMS AT $3 PER ACRE!
And not a foot of waste land
FARMS ON TEN YEAR'S CREDIT
And on purchase no portion of the principal required! !

---

[25] *The Shaping of the Modern Mind* (New York: New American Library of World Literature, Inc., 1953), p. 14.
[26] *Understanding History* (New York: Alfred A. Knopf, Inc., 1950), p. 269.

LANDS NOT TAXABLE FOR SIX YEARS!
Farming Lands in
Eastern Kansas
But one hour's ride from the city of
Atchison and the Missouri River are
offered on terms which guarantee to the
actual settler larger benefits than can be
secured under The Homestead Act.
THE CENTRAL BRANCH
UNION PACIFIC RAILROAD CO.
Offer for sale their lands in the celebrated
Kickapoo Indian Reservation
152,417 Acres.
SCHOOLS AND CHURCHES
FREE FROM TAXATION FOR SIX YEARS! [27]

The family is gathered around the fire, and the poster is read. At this point the teacher asks, "What do you suppose the family will do?" The quick and almost universal reaction is usually something like, "They'd move west to Kansas!" The teacher might then suggest they try acting out the story, with different people in the class playing the roles of various members of the family. Each volunteer is given one of these descriptions on a 3 x 5 card:

Grandfather: You are old, very tired. You brought your family here from Europe years ago. You settled in this village and raised your family here. Your wife died and was buried here and it is the dearest place in the world to you . . .

Father: The farm is failing; in another year you will have to sell it and try to get some kind of job. You have always wanted a large fertile farm of your own—perhaps more than anything else in the world . . .

Mother: You know the farm is not doing very well. You think we probably should go to Kansas, yet you are not sure that everything in the poster is really true. You are doubtful—you want proof . . .

Eldest Son: Adventure and excitement are the most important things in your life. You can't wait to get started . . .

Eldest Daughter: You are very much in love with a boy on the next farm. You hope to marry him in a few years. You do not want to go . . .

---

[27] In Marshall B. Davidson, *Life in America* (Boston: Houghton Mifflin Company, 1951), I, 286. Courtesy Railway & Locomotive Historical Society.

10 Year Old Girl: You are a sickly child who can't bear traveling, roughing it. You love peace, quiet, books, and the comfort of home . . .

When the play is finally dramatized, the decision often turns out to be far more difficult than the children first imagined. Alternative choices *are* considered, and the class's oversimplified image of the past is, to some extent, corrected. Following the dramatization and discussion of the *hypothetical* situation described above, the teacher might read sections of Hamlin Garland's *A Son of the Middle Border*. This authentic and exciting account of a *real* family's decision to move west (and the consequences of that decision) includes passages like the following:

> "Well, Dick," Grandad began, "so ye're plannin' to go west, air ye?"
> "Yes, as soon as I get all my grain and hogs marketed I'm going to pull out for my new farm over in Iowa."
> "Ye'd better stick to the old coulee," warned my grandfather, a touch of sadness in his voice. "Ye'll find none better."
> My father was disposed to resent this. "That's all very well for the few who have the level land in the middle of the valley," he retorted, "but how about those of us who are crowded against the hills? You should see the farm I have in Winneshiek! Not a hill on it big enough for a boy to coast on. It's right on the edge of Looking Glass Prairie, and I have a spring of water, and a fine grove of trees just where I want them, not where they have to be grubbed out."
> "But ye belong here," repeated Grandfather. "You were married here, your children were born here. Ye'll find no such friends in the west as you have here in Neshonoc. And Belle will miss the family."
> My father laughed. "Oh, you'll all come along. Dave has the fever already. Even William is likely to catch it."
> Old Hugh sighed deeply. "I hope ye're wrong," he said. "I'd like to spend me last days here with me sons and daughters around me, sich as are left to me," here his voice became sterner. "It's the curse of our country,—this constant moving, moving. I'd have been better off had I stayed in Ohio, though this valley seemed very beautiful to me the first time I saw it." [28]

Similarly, Laura Ingalls Wilder's easy to read diary, *On The Way Home*,[29] is an unusually effective source of straightforward, descriptive material about a real family's late nineteenth century journey from South Dakota to Missouri.

---

[28] Hamlin Garland, *A Son of the Middle Border* (New York: The Macmillan Company, 1917), pp. 61–62.
[29] New York: Harper & Row, Publishers, 1962.

Another approach that offers possibilities at various grade levels involves the use of historical fiction. Assuming his class is studying the American Revolution, the teacher might ask the students to imagine for a moment that they are living in Lexington, Massachusetts, in the year 1775. A breathless, excited young rider has just reined in his horse in the middle of the village common, and a crowd has quickly gathered. At this point, the teacher could read to his class the following excerpts from Howard Fast's *April Morning*, a stirring and detailed account of the events that took place on April 19, 1775, in and around Lexington. The rider is answering the crowd's worried questions:

"Now just one thing," . . . "just one thing—what time did they start?"

"I told you they were getting into boats to cross the Charles at ten o'clock."

"That's three hours ago. Did you wait until they crossed the river? How long did it take them?"

"I waited until the first of them set onto dry land, I did—and they were forming up on the Menotomy Road. We just decided not to wait any longer."

.   .   .   .

"Did you come straight here?" The Reverend asked.

"By the Lord, I did, hell for leather—and I like to broke my neck on the pitch-black road. I'm here, ain't I? But I can't sit here all night. There was four of us, and one took off for Medford and another for Brookline and the third down to Watertown. You see, the meaning of it was that, one road or another, they'd be going to Concord where the stores are. Someone played the dirty rat and informed that the Committees were stashing away whatever they could put their hand on at Concord, so however they're coming, you can believe me that Concord is where they're headed at."

.   .   .   .

". . . How many troops? . . . weve got to know . . ."

"Mister, it was nighttime and we were hiding. Did you want me to count them?"

"A thousand—two thousand?"

"A thousand at least. Maybe two thousand, maybe more. They had a line of boats stretching across the river, and every boat packed full of redcoat soldiers. That's all I know—Now, make way for me. Let go of my reins, mister." [30]

Before proceeding further, the teacher might ask the class to make some guesses about the possible reactions of the colonists, the courses of

---

[30] From *April Morning*, pp. 58–60, by Howard Fast. Copyright 1961 by Howard Fast. Used by permission of Crown Publishers, Inc.

action they *could* follow. Regardless of the class's responses, however, the initial reading should be followed by Fast's description of the discussion as it probably took place that night:

> At the center of the dispute were four positions: Jonas Parker wanted an immediate muster of the militia. Since we had stored a hogshead of powder and another of lead shot in the cellar of Buckman's Tavern, Parker suggested that as our mustering point . . .
>
> . . . .
>
> [Cooper] on the other hand, resisted a militia muster. It was incumbent upon him to take an antimilitarist position, and he bolstered his argument by suggesting the dangers of arming every sleepy citizen in the vicinity. Someone was bound to get hurt. Instead, he pressed for a Committee meeting in the church . . .
>
> . . . .
>
> The Reverend's position was that before we did anything, we should check the facts. I had half-suspected that he might put in a bid for a long prayer meeting, but all he desired was a practical approach to the problem . . .
>
> . . . .
>
> Sam Hodley stated the fourth position, that it was much ado about nothing, and not for a minute did he believe a wild tale about a British army marching up from Boston. It made no sense, he said. Anybody who knew the British knew that they didn't march at night . . .[31]

A discussion of this material should help the class recognize that this was, of course, an "open question"; what to do—whether to fight, negotiate, flee, stand unless fired upon, etc.—had to be decided by the people of Lexington that day, at that point in time. They were unaware that what they did that day would "make history."

To further emphasize the openness of the future—the complexity of deciding now, for our time, what should or shouldn't be done, students from upper elementary through senior high school might list a series of significant current problems. For example, senior high school students might choose issues such as "What to do about Vietnam," "What to do about the Congo," "Should we remain in the U.N.?" "Should we continue the nuclear test ban treaty?" "Should we admit Communist China to the U.N." etc. Over a period of time, the students could study newspapers, magazines, and other sources, looking wherever possible for differing suggestions, proposals, or alternative plans of action—particularly those based upon what has happened in the past. Each problem should have the proposed "solutions" listed under it, and the longer the list, the better. A careful evaluation of many of the proposed solutions will reveal that

---

[31] *Ibid.*, pp. 61–62.

most of them depend upon history for their validation. Concerning the Vietnam question, for example, history tells us that allowing aggressors to infiltrate and take over a country generally whets the aggressor's appetite rather than satiating it; on the other hand, history also tells us that most Asian people resent interference by Western powers. History tells us, too, that the use of more and more force in situations like Vietnam is often met with more force by the enemy, and that it is difficult, indeed, to win a war without the support of the people. If, for the moment, the class attempts to put itself either singly or collectively into the role of "decision-maker," the difficulty of deciding which view is right or, better still, what history tells us to do should become clear. Similarly, students might evaluate the problems that confronted leaders like Washington, Lincoln, Wilson, Truman, Kennedy, and others. All faced difficult decisions, and all had a number of alternatives from which to choose.

Perhaps no event in recent times illustrates the lack of obvious historical inevitables or immutable laws as they relate to modern day power politics and decision making better than does the Cuban crisis of 1961–62. Senior high school students, using periodicals and newspapers in particular, might easily reconstruct those critical days of October, 1962. The class might first attempt to list some of the possible courses of action open to the President and his advisors. These were undoubtedly among the suggestions considered:

1. Bring the entire matter to the UN.
2. Destroy the missiles by an immediate surprise air strike.
3. Send troops in large enough numbers to guarantee a successful invasion.
4. Block off Cuba's supply lines through an embargo or "quarantine."
5. Allow Cuba to retain the missiles, but make it clear that no further penetration of the Western hemisphere will be tolerated by the United States.

The students should, in each case, weigh the possible Russian reaction to each of the courses of action suggested. In particular, the class might attempt (largely through studies of newspapers published from about October 15 until November 1, 1962) to assess the mood of the country—the fear, the uncertainty that existed among so many of our people. At that point, few Americans were willing to state with any degree of certainty that they knew exactly what the Russians would do—that history made it clear what their response would be, etc. As the class studies the final decision to blockade Cuba and intercept missile-carrying Russian ships, the massive sigh of relief which greeted the Russian decision to turn back her ships and avoid a clash of arms might well be underscored. Apparently a wise decision had been made, and American strategy had worked; but anyone reading contemporary accounts of the incident would surely conclude that our action was anything but guaranteed by history, and that any number of variables could conceivably have altered our decision to act or the Russians' decision to withdraw.

For many people history has apparently acted as a barrier to creative thought rather than as a catalyst for new ideas. Another way of helping students at various age levels understand the positive possibilities that have existed in every age (if only man has the vision to see them) is to examine statements made by well-meaning, but visionless individuals who based their conception of the future only in terms of the "conventional wisdom" of their time. Assuming the class has already studied topics such as the invention of the airplane, television, the electric light, and the telephone, or key events such as the American Revolution, the desegregation of schools, the development of the social security program, free compulsory education for all, etc., the teacher might put the following heading on the chalkboard or on a mimeographed assignment sheet:

What Does History Tell Us?

Under this heading, questions like these might be listed:

1. Will man be able to fly in heavier-than-air craft?
2. Will man be able to send pictures through the air over vast distances?
3. Will man be able to light an entire city by the flick of a switch?
4. Will Americans be able to provide free public education for all?
5. Will Americans see to it that all races attend school on a non-segregated basis?
6. Will the American colonies be able to defeat England and gain their freedom?

Committees or groups of students might choose one question each for further investigation. In each case, however, they are to attempt to answer the question (citing historical evidence) not as people living in the second half of the twentieth century, but rather as if they were living at various times in the past. For example, the group that chooses the question related to man's ability to fly would assume they were living and studying in the year 1900. Having marshalled all the evidence, what *does* history tell us? Obviously, at that point, most "authorities" remained unconvinced that heavier-than-air flight was possible; yet, a short time later, the Wright brothers made their historic flight. The group investigating the question dealing with the possibility of integrated schools might also imagine they were living in 1900. The evidence they put together, including perhaps the famous *Plessy* vs. *Ferguson* decision of the Supreme Court in 1896, would undoubtedly indicate that such schools were not a possibility; yet, by 1954, the same court had seen fit to reverse that decision, and, little by little, integrated schools are becoming a reality in all parts of the United States.

The group concerned with the possibility of the thirteen colonies defeating Great Britain might imagine they were living in the year 1750. At that time the thought of the colonies defeating a power like England seemed remote, indeed, and an objective look at comparative military and naval strength, experience, equipment, etc., would surely indicate that any such unequal struggle almost inevitably would lead to a disastrous defeat for the colonies. Yet other factors grew in significance as time went on, and the impossible became reality.

As each question is investigated it should become clear that history does not tell us what to do. Man, in each new generation and in each new age, re-evaluates his situation and often does what, to an older generation, seemed completely beyond the realm of possibility.

Another more positive means of dealing with the concept of "open-endedness" in history involves an examination of some of the giants of the past who were able to see beyond the limitations of "what is" and "what was" and use their knowledge of the past as a means of developing a fuller life for all. John F. Kennedy's *Profiles in Courage* [32] is filled with examples of individuals who defied convention and tradition and went on, often at great personal sacrifice, to make significant contributions to the betterment of their country. These were individuals who had both a sense of the past and a sense of its meaning for the future.

In the prologue to Sidney Kingsley's play, *The Patriots,* there is a classic example of an "historical giant" in action—an example with profound implications for our own time as well. It concerns Thomas Jefferson. We find him standing on the deck of a schooner headed for America. It is 1790. In a vision, Jefferson recalls the writing of the Declaration of Independence. The voice of a Mr. Reid rises in objection:

REID'S VOICE. That second sentence. Don't like it.

JEFFERSON. But that is the heart of it, man. Are we going to have to creep up on liberty, inch by inch?

REID'S VOICE. Where does this lead? No wonder we're driving all our men of property into the arms of the loyalists.

JEFFERSON. I was asked to write the declaration and I wrote it. I haven't tried to be original. This is a simple expression of the American mind. Our people want this.

---

[32] New York: Pocket Books, Inc., 1957.

REID'S VOICE. From a legalistic viewpoint . . .

JEFFERSON. The men who migrated to America, who built it with their sweat and blood were laborers, not lawyers.

REID'S VOICE. Plague on't, boy! You want some precedent. Where can you show me anything like this in history?

JEFFERSON. Where in history do we see anything like this new world or the man of this new world? Where have we ever seen a land so marked by destiny to build a new free society based on the rights of man? Precedent? Let's make precedent! Better to set a good example, than follow a bad one.[33]

Benjamin Franklin, too, saw in history not an inevitable series of clashes and catastrophes but rather a vision of the possibilities for the good life that existed on the earth. In 1783 he wrote this message to a friend:

Benjamin Franklin to Joseph Banks.

Passy, July 27, 1783

I join with you most cordially in rejoicing at the return to peace. I hope it will be lasting, and that mankind will at length, as they call themselves reasonable creatures, have reason and sense enough to settle their differences without cutting throats; for, in my opinion, *there never was a good war or a bad peace.* What vast additions to the conveniences and comforts of living might mankind have acquired, if the money spent in wars had been employed in works of public utility! What an extension of agriculture, even to the tops of our mountains; what rivers rendered navigable or joined by canals; what bridges, aqueducts, new roads and other public works, edifices and improvements, rendering England a complete paradise, might have been obtained by spending those millions in doing good which in the last war have been spent in doing mischief; in bringing misery into thousands of families, and destroying the lives of so many thousands of working people, who might have performed the useful labor! . . .[34]

Upper elementary, junior, and senior high school students might contrast Franklin's letter with significant modern documents such as the nuclear test ban treaty, the Declaration of Human Rights, or perhaps these excerpts from the Charter of the United Nations:

WE THE PEOPLES OF THE UNITED NATIONS DETERMINED

TO SAVE SUCCEEDING GENERATIONS FROM THE scourge of war, which twice in our lifetime has brought untold sorrow to mankind, and

---

[33] Sidney Kingsley, *The Patriots* (New York: Random House, Inc., 1943). Reprinted by permission.

[34] Bigelow (ed.), *Works of Franklin*, X, 147–48, in Henry Steele Commager and Richard B. Morris (eds.), *The Spirit of Seventy-Six: The Story of the American Revolution as Told by Participants* (Indianapolis: The Bobbs-Merrill Co., Inc., 1958), II, 1274–1275.

to reaffirm faith in fundamental human rights, in the dignity and worth of the human person, in the equal rights of men and women and of nations large and small, and

to establish conditions under which justice and respect for the obligations arising from treaties and other sources of international law can be maintained, and

to promote social progress and better standards of life in larger freedom,

AND FOR THESE ENDS

to practice tolerance and live together in peace with one another as good neighbors, and

to unite our strength to maintain international peace and security, and

to ensure, by the acceptance of principles and the institution of methods, that armed force shall not be used, save in the common interest, and

to employ international machinery for the promotion of the economic and social advancement of all peoples,

HAVE RESOLVED TO COMBINE OUR EFFORTS TO ACCOMPLISH THESE AIMS.

Accordingly, our respective Governments, through representatives assembled in the city of San Francisco, who have exhibited their full powers found to be in good and due form, have agreed to the present Charter of the United Nations and do hereby establish an international organization to be known as the United Nations.[35]

The focal point for discussion here ought to be the idea that war is not inevitable; that, despite the record of wars throughout history, there is no law that says war has to occur, and we in our time (as have people in all times) have the opportunity to choose either a new way or the old.

3. *Ideally, the Past Should Be Understood on Its Own Terms. Historical Events Should Be Examined in Light of the Standards, Values, Attitudes, and Beliefs That Were Dominant During a Given Period and for a Given People, Rather Than Evaluated Exclusively by Twentieth-Century Standards.*

. . . To judge earlier societies by more advanced codes of ethics; to expect balanced judgments and normal conduct in times of war, revolution, or upheaval; to translate the folkways, conventions, and standards

---

[35] David Cushman Coyle, *The United Nations and How It Works* (New York: Mentor Books, New American Library of World Literature, Inc., 1960), pp. 183–184.

of one country to another; to condemn an individual's act without attempting to comprehend his norms or environment; to be intolerant of an "ignorance" which is in fact a comprehensive knowledge of and a healthy adjustment to a different culture—these and other failures to place persons and events in their own historical setting would often lead to failure to understand the surviving documents and nearly always to misjudgments of the personalities and mores of that setting.[36]

Each generation has tampered in some way with the fundamental standards, values, and beliefs of its predecessors. This tampering has a cumulative effect, and when one goes back three, four, or more generations in time, changes in behavioral patterns become more and more pronounced. Thus it becomes increasingly difficult to view human events and activities of another era in an entirely objective way. Our twentieth century culture gets in the way when we attempt to study the past just as our Western culture does when we attempt to study non-Western civilizations. Historian Edward H. Carr stated the problem in the most specific of terms when he wrote:

> Much of what has been written in English-speaking countries in the last ten years about the Soviet Union, and in the Soviet Union about the English-speaking countries, has been vitiated by this inability to achieve even the most elementary measure of imaginative understanding of what goes on in the mind of the other party. . . . History cannot be written unless the historian can achieve some kind of contact with the mind of those about whom he is writing.[37]

Teachers in the intermediate grades could begin to develop this understanding through a study of the settling of the new world. The teacher might suggest that the class imagine they are about to make a trip similar to that made by Englishmen coming to Jamestown, Virginia, in 1607. They are going to a wilderness; there will be no stores, no supermarkets, no drug stores. They will not get any help for months. It is now about a month before sailing and they are making out a list of the food, clothing, tools, arms, and household items that would be absolutely essential for survival in the new world. At this point the teacher could either have the class make individual lists of items and then pool their ideas or simply record items on the chalkboard as the children mention them. When the class has listed everything that seems essential to them, the teacher could suggest they carefully examine the following list. These were the items usually brought over by new settlers of this

---

[36] Louis Gottschalk, *op. cit.*, p. 136.

[37] Edward H. Carr, *What Is History?* (New York: Alfred A. Knopf, Inc., 1964), p. 27.

period. (This data is taken from an original document first published in London in 1622.)[38]

Apparell

One Monmouth Cap
Three shirts
One waste-coate
One suite of Canvase
One suite of Frize
One suite of Cloth

Apparrell   Three paire of Irish stockins
for one   Foure paire of shooes
man   One paire of garters
One paire of Canvase sheets
Seven ells of Canvase, to make a bed and boulster
One Rug for a bed which with the bed serving for two men
Five ells coarse Canvase, to make a bed at sea for two men, to be filled with straw
One coorse rug at sea for two men

Victuall

Eight bushels of meale

For a   Two bushels of pease
whole   Two bushels of Oatemeale
year for   One gallon of Aguavite
one man   One gallon of Oyle
Two gallons of Vinegar

Armes

One Armour compleat, light
One long peece, five foot or five and a halfe, neere Musket bore

For one   One sword
man   One belt
One bandaleere
Twenty pound of powder
Sixty pound of shot or lead, Pistoll and Goose shot

Tooles

Five broadhowes
Five narrow howes
Two broad axes
Five felling Axes
Two Steel hand sawes
Two two-hand sawes
One whipsaw
Two hammers

---

[38] In Davidson, *op. cit.*, I, 51. By permission of the John Carter Brown Library, Brown University.

For a
family
of 6
Three shovels
Two spades
Two augers
Sixe chissels
Two percers
Three gimlets
Two hatchets
Two hand-bills
One grindlestone
Nailes of all sorts
Two pickaxes

Household Implements
One Iron Pot
One kettle
For a   One large frying pan
family   One gridiron
of 6   Two skillets
One Spit
Platters, dishes, spoones of wood

The teacher might then ask his class to cross off the items on *their* list that also appear on the "original" list or chart. All left-over items could be included in a list of articles *we* thought were essential but that the early settlers probably didn't taken along. Since the class usually suggests many items that the colonists didn't have, the teacher might ask how many (if they had the chance) would have been willing to go on such a voyage? We might expect at this point that a note of caution would have crept into the class's attitude; i.e., if the Jamestown settlers took so few "essential" items, embarking on a voyage like this might be far more dangerous and uncomfortable than *we* would like to experience. The teacher could then suggest that the children imagine they were suddenly able to examine a cottage that was typical of those inhabited by many Englishmen around 1620. How many items on our "class list" might there be in the cottage? A careful study of the "class list" should reveal that a number of items thought essential by those of us living in the twentieth century were not available to the Jamestown settlers or to anyone else living in early seventeenth century England. This point could be elaborated on through questions like these:

1. If Mary Jones, U.S. citizen of the twentieth century, were to make the trip with only the original list of supplies, would it seem more or less difficult for her than for Priscilla Evans, English citizen of the seventeenth century?

2. Who do you think would suffer the most? Why?
3. Would there be some hardships that might be about the same for both Mary and Priscilla?

Hopefully, the class would begin to understand that while *both* would find it hard to leave friends, relatives, and familiar places, our twentieth century standards of comfort and convenience would make such a trip seem almost impossibly hard for us, while an individual living during the seventeenth century would judge the hardships of the trip only in terms of general living conditions as they existed at that time.

Another method that could be used with primary children involves the use of pictorial material or other items from the past. Even first and second graders, for example, might be shown pictures of the way people used to live in their community: pictures of automobiles of a generation or two ago, pictures of clothes that once were fashionable, cutouts of old magazines or Sears catalogs, perhaps some real shoes or boots or other items that may have been stored in someone's attic, etc. A display of such pictures and items might be made, and the teacher could discuss each with the class, alerting himself in particular for comments and reactions indicating ridicule or derision on the part of the children.

At this point, some simple dramatic play might be employed. One child could be the mother, while two or three are "children." The scene is the living room of a modern home. The mailman has just delivered the new spring Sears Roebuck catalog. Mother and children look through the catalog for items they would most like to buy. Perhaps a few groups of children might enjoy acting out the event, looking for different items that appeal to them. Eventually, the teacher might suggest that they try this again—but this time we will imagine we are living a long time ago—perhaps 50 or 100 years. Mother and children are seated in the living room and a brand new catalog of *that* period is delivered. Discussion could then be stimulated through questions like these:

1. How do you think the people will behave?
2. Will they laugh at the things in the catalog as some of you did earlier? Why or why not?
3. What made some of us think these older things were "funny"?
4. Do you think people some day will think some of our things were "funny"? Why?

Similarly, older children might enjoy discussing the following headline, which appeared in the May 22, 1927, edition of the *New York Times*.

LINDBERGH DOES IT! TO PARIS IN 33½ HOURS; FLIES
1,000 MILES THROUGH SNOW AND SLEET; CHEERING
FRENCH CARRY HIM OFF FIELD.

Obviously, 33½ hours from New York to Paris is hardly likely to
stir today's jet-age children who are well aware of the existence of five-
or six-hour transatlantic flights. Nevertheless, the headline is real and
the people's reactions were real. For them to respond this way, certain
conditions had to exist, and it should be a fairly simple matter for the
class to deduce that Lindbergh's flight was probably the first of its kind,
that until that time crossing the ocean took many days by steamer, that
this flight had somehow made their world a little smaller. If one puts
oneself in the role of a citizen living in 1927, the excited, enthusiastic
response that greeted the news of Lindbergh's flight can be easily understood; indeed, a realistic appraisal of the response of people all over the
world to the Lindbergh flight demands that we attempt to view their
reactions in terms of the conditions that existed at the time of the event
rather than through the eyes of a "Monday morning quarterback" living
40 or 50 years later.

The difficulties involved in evaluating or judging the past through
the eyes of those who lived it may be handled in still another way.
Intermediate or junior high school students studying the Civil War,
for example, might be asked to write down their guesses concerning the
average age of soldiers who fought in that war. While a variety of
guesses might be made, one would expect that some figure in the early
twenties would represent a class consensus. The teacher might also ask
the class to suggest possible minimum or maximum ages as well as the
reasons for such restrictions. We might expect students to support their
hypotheses with statements such as these:

Boys under a certain age had to go to school.
It isn't right for children to fight in wars.
You aren't strong enough to march, fight, train, etc., until you're at
least .... years old.
We believe that only full-grown, healthy young men should serve in the
armed forces.
Until you're grown up you shouldn't be away from home and parents.
The government would never allow it, etc., etc.

The teacher could then present his class with the following chart
indicating the actual ages of many of the "men" who fought in the
Civil War. (The average age, incidentally, was 19.)

About 844,000 were 17 years old and under
About 231,000 were 16 years old and under
About 100,000 were 15 years old and under
About   1,500 were 14 years old and under
About   300 were 13 years old and under
About   278 were 12 years old and under

Since the actual figures will undoubtedly clash with many guesses made by the class, the teacher might suggest they concentrate on attempting to explain their inaccurate guesses as well as list some of the conditions which permitted so many children to take part in the war. Again, the class might conclude that their image of a soldier is based upon modern conditions, attitudes, and beliefs, and their guesses about the Civil War were largely inaccurate because they were judging in terms of today rather than yesterday.

The study of history offers the perceptive teacher a virtually endless series of events, occurring in a great variety of times and places, that can help students at almost any age level to understand this generalization. Without attempting to classify them as far as age or grade level is concerned, the following samples of contemporary drawing and writing seem especially suited to this kind of investigation and study.

Marshall Davidson, in Volume I of his fascinating *Life in America,* includes some drawings and written descriptions of sea-monsters that were thought to exist during the fourteenth and even fifteenth centuries— monsters that might put a quick and horrible end to the voyage of a seaman who wandered too far from the regularly travelled waterways. As students study the voyages of the many courageous and ambitious men who began to broaden man's vision of the world in which he lived during the fifteenth century, they might be asked to examine such drawings. While some students will, of course, scoff at the ignorance that led some men to accept the existence of such creatures, the teacher should move beyond this point and suggest that his class attempt to hypothesize or offer possible explanations for such beliefs. In other words, what conditions might have existed at that time to make the existence of such creatures plausible? Students may come up with responses like these:

1. At that time people didn't know as much about sailing ships as we do, ships were smaller, many ships never returned home, and people didn't know exactly why. They might have blamed some of this on "monsters."

2. People had no radios or newspapers. Few people could read, so news was told and passed on from person to person, and wasn't always accurate.
3. People had superstitions about a lot of things besides sea-monsters. They probably seemed possible to them.
4. Man had not explored very much of the earth's surface, and little was known about it.
5. There were few schools, and many people had little or no education.

Similarly, high school students might analyze the conditions that made this letter, written by a Spanish physician to his son during the fourteenth century, sound entirely reasonable and sensible to the people of his time:

> Beware of eating too much and too often, especially during the night. Avoid eating raw onions in the evening except rarely, because they dull the intellect and senses generally.
>
> . . . Beware of eating milk and fish, or milk and wine, at the same meal for milk and fish or milk and wine produce leprosy.
>
> Don't sleep in winter with cold feet, but first warm them at the fire or by walking about or some other method. And in summer don't sleep with bed slippers on your feet, because they generate vapors which are very bad for the brain and memory.
>
> Don't go straight to bed on a full stomach but an hour after the meal; also, unless some urgent necessity prevents, walk about for a bit after a meal, at least around the square, so that the food may settle in the stomach and not evaporate in the mouth of the stomach, since the vapors will rise to the head and fill it with rheum and steal away the cut short memory. . . .
>
> Also in summer, in order not to have fleas or to have no more of them, sweep your room daily with a broom and not sprinkle it with water, for they are generated from damp dust. But you may spray it occasionally with strong vinegar which comforts heart and brain.[39]

In the New Orleans of 1825, the selling and bartering of Negroes was considered a perfectly normal, reasonable procedure. While some Americans of that time were extremely critical of the practice; most accepted it as part of a "way of life." While such practices are quickly condemned as primitive by almost all twentieth century Americans, it is, nevertheless, a worthwhile exercise to put oneself in the role of a Southern citizen of that period and attempt to list the values, attitudes,

---

[39] Leon Bernard and Theodore R. Hodges, *Readings in European History* (New York: The Macmillan Company, 1958), pp. 147–149.

beliefs, and rationalizations that make such behavior seem reasonable. This handbill, advertising a New Orleans slave auction, could provide some of the raw material to spark a discussion of this kind.

THE OWNER OF THE FOLLOWING NAMED AND VALUABLE SLAVES, BEING ON THE EVE OF DEPARTURE FOR EUROPE, WILL CAUSE THE SAME TO BE OFFERED FOR SALE, AT THE NEW EXCHANGE, CORNER OF ST. LOUIS AND CHARTRESS STREETS, ON SATURDAY MAY 16, AT TWELVE O'CLOCK, VIZ.

1. SARAH, a mulatress, aged 45 years, a good cook and accustomed to house work in general, is an excellent and faithful nurse for sick persons, and in every respect a first rate character.
2. DENNIS, her son, a mulatto, aged 24 years, a first rate cook and steward for a vessel. Having been in that capacity for many years on board one of the Mobile packets; is strictly honest, temperate, and a first rate subject.
3. CHOLE, a mulatress, aged 36 years, she is without excption, one of the most competent servants in the country, a first rate washer and ironer, does up lace, a good cook, and for a bachelor who wishes a house-keeper she would be invaluable; she is also a good ladies maid, having travelled to the north in that capacity.
4. FANNY, her daughter, a mulatress, aged 16 years, speaks French and English, is a superior hair-dresser (pupil of Gulliac,) a good seamstress and ladies' maid, is smart, intelligent, and a first rate character.
5. DANDRIDGE, a mulatoo, aged 26 years, a first rate dining-room servant, a good painter and rough carpenter, and has but few equals for honesty and sobriety.
6. NANCY, his wife, aged about 24 years, a confidential house servant, good seamstress, mantuamaker and tailoress, a good cook, washer and ironer, etc.
7. MARY ANN, her child, a creole, aged 7 years, speaks French and English, is smart, active and intelligent.
8. FANNY OR FRANCES, a mulatress, aged 22 years, is a first rate washer and ironer, good cook and house servant, and has an excellent character.
9. EMMA, an orphan, aged 10 or 11 years, speaks French and English, has been in the country 7 years, has been accustomed to waiting on table, sewing etc; is intelligent and active.
10. FRANK, a mulatto, aged about 32 years, speaks French and English, is a first rate hostler and coachman, understands perfectly well the management of horses, and is, in every respect, a first rate character, with the exception that he will occasionally drink, though not a habitual drunkard.

All the above named slaves are acclimated and excellent subjects; they were purchased by their present vendor many years ago, and will therefore be severally warranted against all vices and maladies prescribed by law, save and except FRANK, who is fully guaranteed in every other respect but the one above mentioned.

TERMS:—One-half cash, and the other half in notes at six months, drawn and endorsed to the satisfaction of the Vendor, with special mortgage on the Slaves until final payment. The Acts of Sale to be passed before WILLIAM BOSWELL, Notary Public, at the expense of the Purchaser.

NEW ORLEANS, MAY 13, 1835.

To most of us today, the idea of witchcraft seems ludicrous; yet there was a time when it seemed quite normal. In 1692, many people in Massachusetts were able to accept the following testimony in a court of law as reasonable and logical. How can we explain the standards, values, and beliefs that made such behavior possible?

QUESTION: "You are here accused for practicing witchcraft . . . [How] do you do it?"

ANSWER: "I cannot tell . . ."

QUESTION: "Do you acknowledge that you are a witch?"

ANSWER: "Yes."

QUESTION: "How long have you been a witch?"

ANSWER: "Not [more than] a week."

QUESTION: "Did the devil appear to you?"

ANSWER: "Yes."

QUESTION: "In what shape?"

ANSWER: "In the shape of a horse."

QUESTION: "What did he say to you?"

ANSWER: "He bid me not to be afraid of any thing . . . but he has proved to be a liar from the beginning."

QUESTION: "Did you . . . at any time . . . ride upon a stick or pole?"

ANSWER: "Yes."

QUESTION: ". . . What sort of worship did you do the Devil?"

ANSWER: "He bid me pray to him and serve him and said he was a god and lord to me."

QUESTION: "What meetings have you been at, at the village?"

ANSWER: "I was once there and Richard Carrier rode with me on a pole, and the Devil carried us." [40]

---

[40] From Thomas Hutchinson, *The Witchcraft Delusion of 1692* (Boston: 1870), in Paul M. Angle, *The American Reader* (Chicago: Rand McNally & Co., 1958), pp. 35–37.

Similarly, students at various age levels could investigate the conditions that would allow an advertisement like this to be published in a New England newspaper during the year 1828.

> Ten or twelve good respectable
> families consisting of 4 or 5
> children each, from 9 to sixteen
> years of age, are wanted to work in a
> cotton mill in the vicinity of Providence.
> Apply to
> William Sprague, Jr.
> at Natick Village.

Finally, teachers of students in the intermediate grades through senior high school might attempt an exercise in creative and historical thinking involving hypothesizing about the future. A class could be asked, for example, to imagine that they are living in the year 2050. They are about to embark upon a cross-country trip, New York to San Francisco. Their specific assignment consists of suggesting ways in which such a trip would be different from a trip taken today; i.e., we might expect a number of improvements in comfort, safety, accommodations, speed, etc. Having projected this image of transportation into the future, the class might, for the moment, assume their hypotheses were correct and that travel in 2050 would, in fact, closely resemble their "educated guesses." As hypothetical citizens of 2050, how, then, would they view modes of transportation that existed back in the 1960's? What might their reactions be to speed limits of 75 miles per hour, current accident rates, the physical shape and appearance of cars, trucks, etc.? Might we not, in fact, appear somewhat primitive if judged solely by the standards of 2050? How would we want our civilization to be judged by future historians? The teacher might build upon this approach by suggesting that the class again project themselves into the future and, this time, react (as citizens of the twenty-first century) to the following series of typical mid-century newspaper headlines and stories:

DEBATE RAGES OVER SUPREME COURT'S DECISION TO
INTEGRATE PUBLIC SCHOOLS

DEFENSE SPENDING TO TOP TEN BILLION THIS YEAR

PRESIDENT INTRODUCES ANTI-POVERTY PROGRAM

STATE LEGISLATURE DECIDES TO RETAIN CAPITAL
PUNISHMENT

RESEARCHERS STILL SEEK CAUSES, CURE FOR CANCER

Obviously, no one can predict with any certainty that cancer will someday be cured, that poverty will be eliminated, or that war will no longer be considered an acceptable means of settling disputes in the future. Nevertheless, all of this *is* possible, and it is probably a worthwhile and somewhat humbling experience to attempt to look at mid-twentieth century conditions through the eyes of an hypothetical, future historian who will probably live in a vastly different world and who, hopefully, will not judge us exclusively by the standards of his time.

4. *Rarely Can Complex Historical Events Be Explained in Terms of a Simple, One-to-One, Cause-and-Effect Relationship. Rather, a Study of the Past Indicates That Multiple-Causation Is the Dominant Pattern.*

. . . The historian, by expanding and deepening his research, constantly accumulates more and more answers to the question: Why? The proliferation in recent years of economic, social, cultural, and legal history—not to mention fresh insights into the complexities of political history, and the new techniques of psychology and statistics—have enormously increased the number and range of our answers. . . .[41]

Among other heinous crimes with which true-false, multiple-choice, matching, and other so-called objective tests deserve to be charged is a monistic, superficial, oversimplified handling of complicated historical events. The fact that some young people and adults have gathered and retained an impression that Luther's *Ninety-Five Theses caused* the Reformation; that the Stamp Tax *caused* the American Revolution; that slavery *caused* the Civil War; and so on should make all of us a bit "gun shy" with respect to our approach to the teaching of history. Certainly, one of the important outcomes of the study of history to which our children and youth can and should be exposed is the understanding that many factors can interact to bring about significant changes in the things man believes, feels, and does.

One way that primary teachers might sensitize their charges to the idea of multiple-causation is to confront children with a group of every-day contemporary events which may have come about as a result of several causes and to stimulate class members to think of as many tenable explanations as possible. For example, the teacher might make the following statement to his class: "Tomorrow we are all going to walk five blocks from our school to see many men and big machines at work. Do you know what they are doing? That's right, they are starting to build a big new elementary school! Did you see all of the old houses

---

[41] Carr, *op. cit.*, pp. 117–118.

being torn down to make a place for the school building? Did you know that we will go to the new school when it is finished and that the building we are in now will be taken down? Why do you think a new school is being constructed?" In this instance, children might suggest points like the following:

1. Our school is very old. It is not as safe as a new one would be.
2. This building is too small for all of the children who go to school here. Maybe more children will be going to school in our neighborhood, too! We have brothers and sisters who will have to have a school to go to. New families are moving into our community.
3. Our school doesn't have a cafeteria or a gym. A bigger school might have these things.
4. This building is not very pretty. The new building will be prettier.
5. All of the kids who go to this school can't play on the playground at the same time. The bigger children push the smaller children around. We need a bigger place to play.
6. Maybe somebody wants to do something else with the land our school building is on. Maybe somebody wants to build another kind of building or a big street or something.
7. This school is noisy. Maybe they want to have a quieter one.
8. Some rooms in our school are too hot in the winter. Some are too cold. Maybe they want to do something about that too.

After the children had tried to offer a variety of explanations, the teacher might provide them with additional information; or they might be encouraged to ask their parents to tell them more about factors contributing to this change. Various historiographers have cautioned students of history to be aware that, while many causes may contribute to a given happening, this does not necessarily imply that all factors are of equal importance. Part of the job of the historian is to weigh the impact of causal elements, to examine their relationships, and to analyze their degrees of influence. In a case similar to the illustration we have used here, the teacher might also ask the children to try to rank the points they have listed in order of importance. (Safety, for instance, would be more significant than some other factors.)

Senior high school students might also enjoy and profit from a problem-solving experience where they would endeavor to identify some possible causes underlying an event that has just taken place in their own community. They could start with a problem such as, "Why was the recent school bond levy defeated?" A group of hypothetical causes such as those listed below could be framed and later informally and partially corroborated or nullified.

The school bond levy was defeated because . . .

(1) It was poorly publicized by its proponents; too few of its potential supporters went to the polls.

(2) People who were for the levy assumed it would pass and stayed home instead of voting.

(3) Local citizens felt that our schools were all right the way they were and that added expenditures were unnecessary.

(4) Any form of additional taxation is unpopular with people these days.

(5) Our community has a large number of senior citizens who voted against the levy because their income is limited.

(6) Etc.

Students would then gather all sorts of data relevant to their problem. They might bring into class such things as posters; newspaper stories, editorials, letters-to-the-editor, and advertisements; scripts used for radio and television voter appeals; and copies of speeches given by proponents and opponents of the levy. They could try to uncover background information on past school levies and related affairs. After carefully working out a few pertinent questions and going over proper interviewing procedure, they could divide up interviewing responsibilities and contact the superintendent of schools, the editor of the local newspaper, home owners, young and old, apartment dwellers in different parts of the city, members of pressure groups working for the passage or defeat of the levy, etc. They would not offer their hunches as "scientific findings," by any means; rather, the emphasis would be on the *number* of causes they could put forth. Class members might also wish to hazard a guess as to the relative importance of various causes they have spotlighted. In any event, young people engaged in this kind of activity would almost surely become wary of a simple cause-effect description of their problem and perhaps of other similar issues.

With students from the third grade through the intermediate grades, the teacher might also give some historic focus to multiple-causation. An event more familiar to the children might be used the first time around. For example, the teacher could ask, "Why did the English settlers come to America?" and then record on the board the ideas and insights of class members. After the suggestions of all the children had been discussed and evaluated, the teacher might show the class a copy of the following "advertisement,"[42] circulated widely in London around 1609:

---

[42] Advertisement courtesy The New York Public Library. This and many other reproductions of documents, posters, handbills, etc., may also be inexpensively obtained from The Pioneer Press, Harriman, Tennessee.

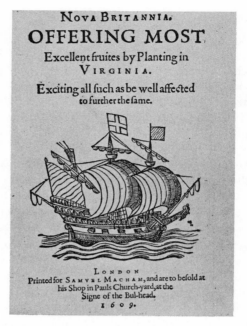

The poster and its appeal might be carefully analyzed, with the teacher explaining the troublesome old-English "s's" that look like "f's" and a few of the more difficult words. Having discussed the particular appeal of primary sources of this kind, the teacher might turn to an appropriate secondary source such as Henry Steele Commager's *The First Book of American History,* which also deals with the teacher's original question. This passage could be used to broaden the class's initial observations:

Why did the settlers come? Why did they venture away from their homes in England, their families and their friends, to take the long trip across the perilous ocean to an unknown world? After all, it was a fearful risk to take. Why then did they keep coming?

For some it was adventure, the thing that still lures people to the far corners of the world, to explore the Arctic or climb the Himalayas or fly into outer space.

For some it was the promise of limitless riches. . . .

Others went out for the glory of their king or queen, to carry the flag of England with them, and plant a New England in America.

Most of them came, however, because they wanted to get away from their Old World and make a fresh start. . . .

There was one other reason why many settlers came to America—a reason that was especially strong with the Pilgrims and the Puritans who came to New England. That was religion. . . .[43]

This same general question—immigration—could be used, of course, with junior and senior high school students in a more detailed fashion and at a higher conceptual level. Following a brief discussion of the causes of immigration, the teacher might read various excerpts such as the one quoted below from the revised and enlarged paperback edition of John F. Kennedy's clearly written and sensitive *A Nation of Immigrants.*

There were probably as many reasons for coming to America as there were people who came. It was a highly individual decision. Yet it can be said that three large forces—religious persecution, political oppression and economic hardship—provided the chief motives for the mass migrations to our shores. They were responding, in their own way, to the pledge of the Declaration of Independence: the promise of "life, liberty and the pursuit of happiness." [44]

A Nation of Immigrants also contains a number of telling illustrations taken from leaflets, drawings, advertisements, lithographs, cartoons, and photographs which could be projected on an opaque projector in class to stimulate an even more empathetic response to the question before the class. The teacher might turn as well to primary materials such as the letters written by immigrants to their relatives in the "Old Country" describing their feelings about their new life and carrying many implications concerning why the move was made. The following letters are representative:

I *own* here a far better estate than I *rented* in England, and am already more attached to the *soil.* Here every citizen . . . is part of the government, identified with it, not *virtually,* but in fact; and eligible to every office . . .[45]

Wages for labor are very high here. A full-grown man can earn from $150 to $160 in wages in one year. Here a poor young man can soon become a well-to-do farmer if he works hard and uses good sense. He can look forward to becoming rich . . . a difficult task in Norway . . .[46]

[43] Henry Steele Commager, *The First Book of American History* (New York: Franklin Watts, Inc., 1957), pp. 6–7.

[44] John F. Kennedy, *A Nation of Immigrants* (New York: Popular Library, Inc., 1964), p. 24.

[45] Morris Birkbeck, *Letters from Illinois* (Philadelphia, 1818), p. 29.

[46] Theodore C. Blegen, *Land of Their Choice* (Minneapolis: University of Minnesota Press, 1955), p. 38.

All kinds of people from all nations of the world live together here like brothers and sisters; and in spite of the fact that there are no garrisons of soldiers, police, and the like, you never hear anything about theft, begging, or any noticeable ill will between neighbors. To me everybody is good, kind, and accomodating. Nobody here can take anything away from you by force . . .[47]

The American treats his employees well; he does not treat them as servants but as his helpers . . .[48]

Here it is not asked, what or who was your father, but the question is, what are you? Freedom seems as essential to every citizen of the United States as the air he breathes . . .[49]

The land in the state of Illinois is largely prairie, with little woodland except along the rivers and creeks. The summers are extremely beautiful. Then the whole country, both woodland and prairie, is bedecked with grass and flowers of all colors, which bloom from earliest spring to late autumn. When some fall, others come up. Some big yellow ones in the autumn have stalks ten feet high. The summer may be compared to an earthly paradise.[50]

In a similar vein, the teacher might read the preamble of the Declaration of Independence, focusing the attention of the class upon the phrase, ". . . requires that they should declare the *causes* which impel them to the separation."[51] Again, with pupils in the intermediate and junior high school grades, the teacher could buttress first reactions of students with the reading of *The Great Declaration* by Henry Steele Commager. This book is filled with excellent materials from diaries, letters, autobiographies, journals, and so on, and contains passages such as this one which should trigger meaningful discussion:

When we ask how the Declaration of Independence came about, and why it was necessary, we are asking big questions. We are indeed asking for a history of the causes of the American Revolution. . . .

Yet by July 1776 the Second Continental Congress voted unanimously for independence. What brought about the change?

Three things. First, it became clear that George III had no intention of meeting the American demands, or of making any important concessions to those he regarded as wicked "rebels." Second, it became clear that if

[47] *Ibid.*, p. 53.
[48] *Ibid.*, p. 86.
[49] Morris Birkbeck, *Notes on a Journey in America* (Philadelphia, 1817), p. 34.
[50] Birkbeck, *Letters from Illinois*, p. 41.
[51] Italics ours.

Americans were united, and could count on some help from France, they had a very good chance to win a war: nobody had quite believed that before Bunker's Hill. And third was the influence of a remarkable pamphlet called *Common Sense* . . . .[52]

Arthur Walworth [53] uses the third volume of Alfonso Toro's *Compendio de Historia de Mexico: La Revolucion de Independencia y Mexico Independiente* to develop the Mexican point of view of the causes of the Texan Revolt. He reports that Toro's book was one of the most widely used of the Mexican histories for the secondary school and that it developed the theme of the land hunger of the United States and placed the blame for hostilities upon the plotting of American imperialists. While Toro's analysis is in itself something of an oversimplification, it does add another dimension to the equally oversimplified version of the origins of the war presented in many American texts. Here, then, are two paragraphs from Toro's book:

> Since a time before Mexico became independent, the United States was desirous of extending its territory at the expense of that of New Spain, to the Rio Grande. They alleged so-called rights, invaded the territory often, and gave rise to frequent claims that never were adequately satisfied . . . .
>
> .   .   .   .
>
> . . . The partisans of the South looked toward us to increase their territory, make new slave states out of it, and strengthen their domination; and they resolutely determined to acquire Texas, counting upon the aid of President Jackson, an unscrupulous man who, as a proprietor of slaves, was personally interested in the matter and resorted to every sort of means, even the most immoral, to accomplish his ends . . . .[54]

Finally, senior high school students in top sections or advanced placement groups might also be challenged to examine the causes of the Civil War. After an entire class has compiled its list of factors contributing to the War Between the States, the teacher might read to them from an extremely interesting and thoughtful paper written by Howard K. Beale which gives an historiographer's approach to this problem. The teacher might begin by sharing with his students this comment by Beale:

---

[52] Henry Steele Commager, writer and ed., *The Great Declaration* (Indianapolis: The Bobbs-Merrill Co., Inc., 1958), p. 18.

[53] *School Histories at War: A Study of the Treatment of Our Wars in the Secondary School History Books of the United States and in Those of Its Former Enemies* (Cambridge, Mass.: Harvard University Press, 1938).

[54] *Ibid.*, pp. 39–40, 41.

. . . Historians have found the causes of the Civil War bafflingly complex. No simple explanation is possible. Early writers found simple answers more satisfying than have later ones. The tendency has been from simple explanations to many-sided ones until recently the picture has become complicated indeed.[55]

One thing that is very clear in Beale's manuscript is not only that there are many causes for the Civil War but that Southern historians on the one hand and Northern historians on the other have assigned different causes over the years. Beale writes that since World War I, historians have tended to shift emphasis from conspiracy, states rights arguments, and slavery to broader social, cultural, ideational, political, economic, and geographic factors. In tracing the work of historians through the decades, he presents this summary of some causes of the Civil War as perceived by earlier Southern writers from 1861 to 1900.

. . . Important factors that brought on the War were: the *Liberator*; anti-slavery societies; irritating activities of the anti-slavery forces in Congress led by John Quincy Adams and Joshua Giddings in the thirties and forties; the organized flood of abolition petitions; formation of the Free-soil Party; efforts to deprive the South of its just gains in the settling of Texas and winning the Mexican War; the persistent reappearance of the Wilmot Proviso; machinations of the New England Emigrant Aid Society; John Brown's activities in Kansas under the Lecompton Constitution; freestate men's refusal to obey the Fugitive Slave Act; successful work of the Underground Railway; personal liberty laws and slave rescues; attacks on the slave trade and slavery in the District of Columbia; anti-Southern activities of anti-slavery clergy, speakers, and press; charges that Southern institutions and Southerners themselves were evil; organization of the Republicans as a sectional party bent on ruining and then ruling the South; Republicans' espousal of the anti-slavery cause; their circulation of *Uncle Tom's Cabin* and Helper's *Impending Crisis*; attacks of Chase, Seward, and Sumner in Congress; Northern refusal to accept the Dred Scott Decision; reputed Republican intention to destroy slavery in the states; the North's greed for power and determination to aggrandize itself; Lincoln's "radical" anti-slavery, anti-Southern attitudes; Lincoln's election with all it implied in Southern minds; Republican defeat of compromise efforts; attempts to provision Sumpter; and Republican determination to "coerce" Southern states. . . .[56]

---

[55] Howard K. Beale, "What Historians Have Said about the Causes of the Civil War," Chapter III in *Theory and Practice in Historical Study: A Report of the Committee on Historiography*, Bulletin No. 54 (New York: Social Science Research Council, 1946), p. 88.

[56] *Ibid.*, p. 58.

While senior high school students may not have time to go into all of the details and ideological conflicts implied in this breathtaking survey, they should at least see that there are indeed many forces which were at work in triggering the Civil War and that one's point of view can color his approach to complex historical events.

5. *The Record of the Past Is Irremediably Fragmentary, Selective, and Biased. The Significance of Available Historical "Facts" Varies With the Individual Who Studies Them, and Each Generation Tends to Recreate and Rewrite History in Terms of Its Own Needs, Aspirations, and Point of View.*

Historians interested in the nature, philosophy, methodology, and writing of history have long concerned themselves with the problems, challenges, and inevitabilities of incompleteness, parochialism, subjectivity and mutability in history. Often, they have openly announced (though sometimes overlooked or glossed over) the obvious fact that they and all historians who will ever follow them can never tell even a significant portion of man's story. They have frequently admitted that their peripheral vision of the world, past and present, has been limited by their experiential bases—constructed of national, regional, religious, philosophical, social, economic, and other components. They have at times acknowledged that their individual perceptions have acted as built-in filters through which all stimuli and data have been strained. And they have granted—with ease for some and difficulty for others—that history itself is subject to change.

If the ability to think reflectively about persistent global concerns of man, contemporary events and issues, and immediate personal problems is one of the appropriate objectives for today's social studies programs, then it would seem to follow that students should learn to think critically about the materials and data they use in and out of the classroom as a part of that aim. Understanding that the historical resources and insights they turn to in their activities and deliberations have been written by men about men and are therefore subject to human errors, shortcomings, perspectives, evaluations, and reconsiderations, they should become increasingly alert to the necessity for resourceful searching and researching and rigorous thinking and rethinking regarding enduring and emerging human questions.

As part of an approach to this fifth fundamental historical insight, the teacher might like to give his students some feeling for the spirit of discovery and rediscovery which can be so much a part of history when it is researched, written, read, interpreted, taught, and discussed in a creative fashion. In a sense, history has a serial, "to-be-continued"—rather than a "finis"—flavor which pupils can learn to savor. Through literature and historical writings teachers can imbue their charges with the sparkle and vital force that energizes the study of this discipline.

In a fascinating, rather haunting passage dealing with the fate of "Injun Joe" in *The Adventures of Tom Sawyer,* Samuel Clemens revealed the feeling he had for history, a feeling which was also evident in other of his works. The teacher of upper-elementary through senior high school might share Clemens' musings with his students to see if they, too, could capture something of this approach—its long view of human affairs, its concern for the timely and the timeless, and its endless search for "whys" regarding man's ideas and actions.

. . . The poor unfortunate had starved to death. In one place near at hand, a stalagmite had been slowly growing up from the ground for ages, builded by the water-drip from a stalactite overhead. The captive had broken off the stalagmite, and upon the stump had placed a stone, wherein he had scooped a shallow hollow to catch the previous drop that fell once in every three minutes with the dreary regularity of a clock-tick—a dessert-spoonful once in four-and-twenty hours. That drop was falling when the Pyramids were new; when Troy fell; when the foundations of Rome were laid; when Christ was crucified; when the Conqueror created the British empire; when Columbus sailed; when the massacre at Lexington was "news." It is falling now; it will still be falling when all these things shall have sunk down the afternoon of history and the twilight of tradition and been swallowed up in the thick night of oblivion. Has everything a purpose and a mission? Did this drop fall patiently during five thousand years to be ready for this flitting human insect's need? And has it another important object to accomplish ten thousand years to come? No matter. It is many and many a year since the hapless half-breed scooped out the stone to catch the priceless drops. . . .[57]

Another literary excerpt which should attract and hold the attention of senior high school students and help them to see how an historian might feel when he comes upon something which serves as a key to unlock new information and insights is the one below, taken from Nathaniel Hawthorne's introduction, "The Custom House," to *The Scarlet Letter.* Hawthorne reports his excitement upon uncovering an old package in the second story of the Custom House, where he worked.

But one idle and rainy day, it was my fortune to make a discovery of some little interest. Poking and burrowing into the heaped-up rubbish in

[57] Samuel L. Clemens, *The Adventures of Tom Sawyer* (New York: The Heritage Press, 1936), pp. 262–263.

the corner . . . I chanced to lay my hand on a small package, carefully done up in a piece of ancient yellow parchment. . . . There was something about it that quickened an instinctive curiosity, and made me undo the faded red tape, that tied up the package, with the sense that a treasure would here be brought to light. . . .

. . . .

But the object that most drew my attention, in the mysterious package, was a certain affair of fine red cloth, much worn and faded. . . . This rag of scarlet cloth . . . assumed the shape of a letter. It was the capital letter A. By an accurate measurement, each limb proved to be precisely three inches and a quarter in length. It had been intended, there could be no doubt, as an ornamental article of dress; but how it was to be worn, or what rank, honor, and dignity, in by-past times were signified by it, was a riddle which . . . I saw little hope of solving. . . .

. . . .

In the absorbing contemplation of the scarlet letter, I had hitherto neglected to examine a small roll of dingy paper, around which it had been twisted. This I now opened, and had the satisfaction to find . . . a reasonably complete explanation of the whole affair. There were several foolscap sheets containing many particulars respecting the life and conversation of one Hester Prynne, who appeared to have been rather a noteworthy personage in the view of our ancestors. She had flourished during the period between the early days of Massachusetts and the close of the seventeenth century. . . . Prying further into the manuscript, I found the record of other doings and sufferings of this singular woman, for most of which the reader is referred to the story entitled "The Scarlet Letter"; and it should be borne carefully in mind, that the main facts of that story are authorized and authenticated by the document of Mr. Surveyor Pue. The original papers, together with the scarlet letter itself,—a most curious relic.—are still in my possession, and shall be freely exhibited to whomsoever, induced by the great interest of the narrative, may desire a sight of them. . . .[58]

Turning to an actual event, the teacher might read to senior high school youth Carl Sandburg's one-volume edition of *Abraham Lincoln: The Prairie Years and the War Years*. This selection illustrates the ever-emergent potentialities of history, the re-examination so often characteristic of this field, the necessity of selection and attendant omission in

---

[58] Nathaniel Hawthorne, *The Scarlet Letter* (New York: Holt, Rinehart & Winston, Inc., 1952), pp. 27–31. The text of *The Scarlet Letter* here given was prepared by Sculley Bradley and first published in *The American Tradition in Literature*, edited by Sculley Bradley, Richmond Croom Beatty, and E. Hudson Long. It is also available in the same editors' Norton Critical Edition of *The Scarlet Letter*, a paperback containing backgrounds, sources, and essays in criticism as well as an annotated text of the novel. Copyright © 1961, 1962 by W. W. Norton & Company, Inc., and here reproduced with their permission.

historical narrative, the incompleteness of any report and analysis dealing with a multi-dimensional topic, and the complexity of the historian's work.

> I have in this work, of course, consulted and made use of such new materials and researches as throw added light on the life and personality of Lincoln. Since the writing of *The Prairie Years* in the early 1920's there have been some thirty years of fiercely intensive research on the life of Lincoln before he became president. In no thirty-year period since the death of Lincoln has so rigorous and thorough an examination been given the facts and myths of the life of Lincoln. . . .
>
> . . . Every biographer of Lincoln is under compulsion to omit all or parts of Lincoln letters and speeches that he would like to include; this in part explains why any Lincoln biography is different from any or all other Lincoln biographies; each must choose and decide what sentences or paragraphs shed the light needed for the Lincoln portrait and story. Supposing all could be told, it would take a far longer time to tell it than was taken to enact it in life.
>
> Here and there exist Lincoln letters not yet published but there are no expectations that they will throw important fresh light. As recently as February 1954 came the first publication of letters of Lincoln to Judge David Davis, which I have used herein as throwing slightly deeper gleams on Lincoln as a master politician. A national event was the opening at midnight on July 26, 1947, the "unveiling" as some termed it, of the long secret Robert T. Lincoln Collection in the Library of Congress. The next five days I did my best at reporting in seven newspaper columns for a syndicate what was revealed in the 18,300 letters, telegrams, manuscripts, miscellaneous data. The fourteen Lincoln scholars and authors present agreed that while no new light of importance was shed on Lincoln, the documents deepened and sharpened the outlines of the massive and subtle Lincoln as previously known. . . .[59]

Secondary students could be challenged as well to find dramatic examples, past and present, of historical research which has had a rather detective-like quality. Individual students, for example, could surely share with their classmates stories such as the one describing the finding and deciphering of the Rosetta Stone which gave the world the key to the lost language of ancient Egypt. A class member might also relate the discovery of the complete text of Quintilian's *Institutes of Oratory.* Petrarch had had access to only a mutilated text of the *Institutio Oratoria.* When the entire manuscript was found in 1416, its discovery was hailed as a great event. A little bit of patient research would uncover the fact

---

[59] Carl Sandburg, *Abraham Lincoln: The Prairie Years and the War Years* (1 vol.; New York: Harcourt, Brace & World, Inc., 1954), pp. vii–viii.

that this work, written in the first century A.D., was very popular with continental Humanists and many others. Men like Erasmus, Luther, Elyot, Mulcaster, Ben Jonson, Pope, and John Stuart Mill were familiar with the *Institutio*. In fact, it received much more attention and was mentioned more frequently during later periods than when it was written. Or, students might find more recent stories and articles which mention historical finds. One such interesting report is "King John's Lost Treasure," written by James Morris and printed in the May 30, 1964, issue of *The Saturday Evening Post*. This passage from the article should give students added feeling for the adventure and vitality which is history:

> Point 467164 on the English Ordnance Survey six-inch map marks a silent and haunting spot in the marsh country of East Anglia on England's North Sea coast. . . .
>
> . . . .
>
> From the subsoil of this desolate place the professor of geology at Nottingham University has extracted a number of curiosities, and if you ask him politely, Prof. William D. Evans may invite you to his laboratories at the university and let you see them. They are small curiosities but undeniably dramatic. And inspected, they have a fine mysterious glitter to them. Some are shreds of silver, minuscule balls or twisted strands; some are glimpses of blue enamel, embedded in lumps of clay; some are small pieces of gold, looking immensely old and fearfully suggestive. Evans shows them to you rather as Merlin might open the cupboard upon Excalibur, and he is justified: For these are, it seems probable, the first relics ever found of the treasure King John of England lost in East Anglia on October 11, 1216.
>
> . . . .
>
> . . . Amateurs have often had a try; historians have painstakingly reconstructed the supposed course of events; but it is only now, seven centuries after the catastrophe, that anyone appears actually to have discovered any trace of the treasure that has excited so many imaginations, inspired so many theories, and kept so many plowboys with their eyes hopefully upon the furrow.[60]

Getting into a few obvious cases of incorrect, slanted, fabricated, or forged documents that historians have detected can be a stimulating and enjoyable experience for senior high school youth. Before launching a short investigation of this fascinating aspect of historical research, the teacher might read this portion of a published dialogue which took place between Arnold Joseph Toynbee, Research Professor Emeritus of Inter-

---

[60] James Morris, "King John's Lost Treasure," *The Saturday Evening Post*, 237, No. 21 (May 30, 1964), 64.

national History at the University of London, and Allen D. Breck, Chairman of the Department of History at the University of Denver:

> BRECK: But the nineteenth-century historians who compiled those incredibly long series of original documents did, indeed, think they had gotten to the real truth of the past.
> TOYNBEE: Yes. They were very naive about documents, weren't they? They thought of documents as if they were geological strata. Documents couldn't lie! Now many documents are made and invented on purpose to lie. Everyone who's worked in the service of any government and has helped to produce such documents knows that documents are not made to tell the truth to historians. They may not be made to tell untruths, but they are always made for some practical purpose, for the sake of action, not of history.[61]

Then, the teacher might read to his class selections from scholars' writings which are concerned with this problem in history and which identify well-known cases of documents that have involved some detective work and about which students could do further reading. Among the sources that might be used for this purpose are Louis Gottschalk's section on "Forged or Misrepresented Documents" in Chapter 3, "External Criticism," of *The Use of Personal Documents in History, Anthropology and Sociology*;[62] Homer Carey Hockett's section on "The Principles of Historical Criticism," in *The Critical Method in Historical Research and Writing*;[63] and Allan Nevins' Chapter 5, "The Cheating Document," in *The Gateway to History*.[64] The following are a few samples familiar to many historians which might be studied by individual students, shared by them with their peers in class, and discussed by class members in the light of the idea being developed here:

1. The Donation of Constantine. (This document was used to substantiate papal territorial claims. Lorenzo Valla demonstrated in 1440 that the Donation was an eighth-century forgery.)
2. Parson Mason Locke Weems's *Life of George Washington*. (This is the folksy, moralistic book which reported the now legendary "cherry tree" story, etc.)
3. Selected Napoleonic materials. (This could include "diaries" composed by others around Napoleon's writings and the letters forged

---

[61] "Dialogue: The Inspirations of Historians," *University of Denver Magazine*, 2, No. 2 (December, 1964), 8.
[62] Louis Gottschalk, Clyde Kluckhohn, and Robert Angell, Bulletin No. 53 (New York: Social Science Research Council, 1945).
[63] New York: The Macmillan Company, 1955.
[64] Nevins, *op. cit.*

by Las Cases, who was Napoleon's companion during the close of the emperor's life.)

4. The "Morey letter." (This was a letter approving the importation of Chinese labor which was attributed falsely to James Garfield in 1880.)

5. The Moabite Pentateuch. (This was conceived by Schapira to defraud the British Museum and was supposed to contain a special version of the Ten Commandments.)

6. A. C. Buell's biography of John Paul Jones. (This two-volume work mixed genuine and fictitious materials.)

7. The Robert Spring forgeries. (This includes hundreds of "documents" counterfeited by a Philadelphia dealer for sale to collectors.)

8. The Lincoln-Rutledge "correspondence." (This is a faked group of letters supposed to have been written by Abraham Lincoln and Ann Rutledge.)

9. The H. L. Mencken history of the bathtub. (This is an article written as a joke which was accepted as fact and later cited in reputable sources.)

The facet of our fifth historical generalization concerned with historiography per se might well be divided into five distinct, significant parts. The first component would be an examination of a given historical event through the eyes of a *single* individual who was involved directly or indirectly in that occurrence while it was taking place. The emphasis here would be on the fact that the individual's background colors his perception of the happening. While countless personal documents—letters, diaries, memoirs, etc.—could be used to get at this initial point, one unusually fine source is *The Diary of George Templeton Strong*, edited by Allan Nevins and Milton Halsey Thomas. Without identifying Strong in any way, the teacher could read numerous comments written by the man on a host of vital national affairs. After the class has been exposed to Strong's perceptions of a multitude of issues, the teacher might then ask questions like the following:

You have heard many excerpts from a diary. What can you guess about the person who wrote these passages?

Was this individual a man or a woman?

Was he or she well educated or poorly educated?

What might this person's occupation have been?

What was his or her financial situation?

Can you suggest something about this writer's political leanings?

From what sources do you think this individual gathered his or her information and opinions?

Was this diarist usually cool, calm, thoughtful, and objective; or was
he or she easily stirred up, given to hasty judgments, and biased?
Can you create an imaginary individual who might have written about
the same events in a different style and with other feelings and
opinions?
Can you think of an actual person who lived at this time and who
might have agreed with a number of the ideas expressed by the person
who wrote the diary from which I have read?
Can you identify a real individual, living during this period, who
might have disagreed with the writer of the diary we have used
in class?
How do *you* feel about the events mentioned in this diary and the
personal philosophy of the man or woman who recorded them?
Why do you agree or disagree with this diarist's thoughts and values?
Where do you get *your* information and *your* attitudes and values?
Would another person be able to guess something about *your* back-
ground by the things you might write about current happenings?
Could *any* individual write about events taking place in his own lifetime with complete objectivity?
Is it possible for an individual to identify some of his limitations and
leanings for himself and others so he and they are at least aware
of personal involvement in all human affairs?
Can a person improve his ability to think and write *more* objectively
about events past and present?
Does all of this discussion that has taken place in our class say anything
to you about history, the writing of history, and your reading of
historical materials?

Following the extended discussion built around questions such as
these, the teacher could provide his students with biographical information about George Templeton Strong and help them check out the
accuracy of their highly subjective analyses of his diary entries. Other
diaries written during this period could also be uncovered and read in
class so the perceptions of Strong could be compared in a more detailed
way with those of his contemporaries. Eventually, this approach might
be culminated with the following invitation given by the teacher to
his students:

We have had an unusually interesting and worthwhile discussion
built around the diary of George Templeton Strong, and we have compared his background and views with those of others who lived at the
same time as revealed in their diaries. Now, I would like to give you a
chance to get into the act! I am inviting each of you to keep a daily
diary for the next two weeks dealing with your summary of and feelings
about events taking place in your community, state, nation, and world.

If this activity appeals to you, you might like to read our weekly current events publications, newspapers, and news magazines; to listen to radio and television newscasts, reports, editorials, analyses, interviews, forums, debates, etc.; and to follow carefully discussions and conversations centered on today's happenings in which others around you are involved and in which you participate at home, school, and elsewhere. If you can do it, you should avoid showing what you are writing in your diary to others or talking about this material with them, for you want to keep this document as personal as possible.

At the end of the two weeks, I would like you to try to analyze what you have written. Ask yourself how much your background has gotten into your summaries and reactions, how objective or biased you have been, and how you might improve your ability to report and examine contemporary events. Then—if you are willing—I would like to have the privilege of reading what you have written and of sharing with your classmates those portions of your diaries which you agree that I may read aloud. I want to respect your privacy in every way, and I will not identify the persons who have written the diaries from which I read. I may skip from diary to diary to read passages which deal with the same happening so you can see various comparisons.

I am going to keep a diary, too, the next two weeks. We will project the things I write on the opaque projector so we can read them together. I will then ask you to try to point out examples of how *my* perceptions of various events have gotten into the "facts" I have set down and my feelings about those "facts."

Finally—after we have concluded this class activity—I hope that some of you will continue to keep your diaries at least for awhile to see if any changes take place in the events you write about and in the way that you view them and write about them.

The second component in this five-part series would be an examination of an event in history through the eyes of *various* individuals who were involved directly or indirectly in that happening while it was occurring and through media other than diaries. The teacher could encourage his charges to identify some significant, substantial, meaningful historical event which would be relevant to the ongoing activities of the class or the given unit then being studied and one for which adequate contrasting material could be obtained. Then—through an examination of speeches, editorials, essays, letters, and the like—the class could compare varied perceptions of the event selected.

Assuming that a class might choose this approach to an issue such as suffrage for women, students will find an abundance of materials revealing various perceptions and perspectives which could be surveyed and discussed. Certainly, one of the sources used would be Susan B. Anthony's speech, "On Woman's Right to Suffrage," which was delivered in 1873 and which ran in part—

Friends and fellow citizens: I stand before you to-night under indictment for the alleged crime of having voted at the last presidential election, without having a lawful right to vote. It shall be my work this evening to prove to you that in thus voting, I not only committed no crime, but, instead, simply exercised my *citizen's rights,* guaranteed to me and all United States citizens by the National Constitution, beyond the power of any State to deny.

. . . it is a downright mockery to talk to women of their enjoyment of the blessings of liberty while they are denied the use of the only means of securing them provided by this democratic-republican government—the ballot.

Webster, Worcester and Bouvier all define a citizen to be a person in the United States, entitled to vote and hold office.

The only question left to be settled now is: Are women persons? And I hardly believe any of our opponents will have the hardihood to say they are not. . . .[65]

This statement was made in the U.S. Senate in 1887:

We have now masses of voters so enormous in numbers as it seems to be almost beyond the power of the law to execute the purposes of the elective franchise with justice, with propriety, and without crime. How much would these difficulties and these intrinsic troubles be increased if we should raise the number of voters from 10,000,000 to 20,000,000 in the United States? That would be the direct and immediate effect of conferring the franchise upon the women.

. . . The effect would be to drive the ladies of the land, as they are termed, the well-bred and well-educated women, the women of nice sensibilities, within their home circles, there to remain, while the ruder of that sex would thrust themselves out on the hustings and at the ballot-box . . . You would paralyze one-third at least of the women of this land by the very vulgarity of the overture made to them that they should go struggling to the polls in order to vote in common with the herd of men.[66]

The third component would be an examination of the same event in history as reported at a *later date* by people involved directly or indirectly in that happening. The purpose of this phase of our five-part

[65] Susan B. Anthony, "On Woman's Right to Suffrage," in Lewis Copeland (ed.), *The World's Great Speeches* (New York: Dover Publications, Inc., 1958), pp. 321–322.
[66] Carrie C. Catt and Nettie R. Shuler, *Woman Suffrage and Politics* (New York: Charles Scribner's Sons, 1926), p. 233.

analysis is to help pupils understand that not only does an individual's perception of an incident shape what he reports and feels about that affair, but also that his initial perception can be blurred, altered, or erased by time.

Most youngsters have played the game where a brief story is first whispered by one child to another and then passed around the group. Inevitably, the story changes by the time the last youngster hears it and repeats his version aloud. There is usually a laugh among the members of the group, then, when the first child retells his original version. This game could be modified easily to get at the idea we wish to convey here. At the beginning of a school day, the teacher could tell a little story to the class, write a very brief account on the board or on the reading chart, or act out something in front of the group. (Or again, an individual child or a small group of pupils could provide the class with a story, report, skit, etc.) Immediately following the exposure of the class to the story or whatever stimulus might be used, the teacher would ask class members to step out into the hall, one at a time, where a tape recorder would be set up and to repeat what they heard or describe what they observed. Then, the recorded accounts of the youngsters would be played to the entire class and discussed. It would be apparent that individual perceptions of children had entered into their taped comments, and this would be underlined by the teacher. The teacher would let a week or so elapse without any mention of this activity. Next, the recording procedure would be repeated with each child trying again to recall the story, report, or skit. The second set of responses would be played aloud in class and compared with the first set of tapings. Then, the members of the class would be asked to offer explanations for differences in the two tapes. Eventually, the teacher could use actual historical materials—chosen to suit interests and abilities of pupils—to show class members how the phenomenon they have experienced enters into written history. For example, with students from the intermediate grades on through the senior high school level the teacher could use portions of Chapter 5, "What Was the Weather at Washington's Inauguration?" from Charles Warren's wonderful book, *Odd Byways in American History*. The appropriateness of this source to our third component is apparent in this comment written by Warren:

> The question as to weather conditions at Washington's Inauguration is a matter of minor importance; but a difference between eyewitnesses on the subject affords an interesting illustration of the unreliability of reminiscences as authority in the writing of history. . . .[67]

---

[67] Charles Warren, *Odd Byways in American History* (Cambridge, Massachusetts: Harvard University Press, 1942), p. 92.

Warren points out that few contemporaneous reports were written about George Washington's inauguration and that the weather was not discussed in any of those descriptions. He says that the first mention of the weather appeared in 1854, sixty-five years after the ceremony. The writer of that narrative, Rufus W. Griswold, was not alive in 1789 and gave no authority for his report; but he had this to say:

> At eight o'clock some clouds about the horizon caused apprehension of an unpleasant day; but when at nine, the bells rung out a merry peal and presently with a slower and more solemn striking called from every steeple for the people to assemble in the churches, to implore the blessing of Heaven on the nation, its favor and protection to the President, and success and acceptance to his Administration, the sun shone clearly down, as if commissioned to give assurance of the approbation of the Divine Ruler of the world.[68]

Warren adds that other more recent authors have written without equivocation that there was sunshine on the day of the first Presidential inauguration, but again that they cite no authority for this statement. Then Warren introduces a description written by Miss Mary Hunt Palmer around 1859. Miss Palmer was fourteen years old in 1789, and was nearly eighty-four years old when she recorded her recollections of the inauguration for her grandchildren. She remembered that

> . . . It never rained faster, I thought, than it did that day. We waited long for the procession. The streets were crowded. At length, a quick movement among them told us it was approaching. It approached, the Father of his Country, bareheaded, only defended by an umbrella, walked at its head. . . . Everyone must have been drenched through that could not find shelter in the neighboring houses. Umbrellas were scarce articles then, and would have been a poor protection at best.[69]

Warren also calls attention to a narrative written in 1821 by Eliza Susan Morton. This lady would have been about sixteen years old in 1789 when she attended the inauguration and forty-eight when she put her recollections on paper. While she did not mention weather conditions in her description, she said that there was a crowd even on the rooftops. Nothing may be found in her statement about rain. All of this leads Warren to comment; "Thus is an interesting problem presented for the historian. Did Miss Morton, writing at the age of forty-eight, forget

---

[68] *Ibid.*, p. 96.
[69] *Ibid.*, p. 99.

about the rain; or did Miss Palmer, writing at the age of eighty-four, remember a rain which never occurred? . . .[70]

The fourth component would be an examination of the same historical event as reported in two different ages. This would help the class to see that the writing of history does change; that new perceptions creep into accounts and analyses; and that "facts" may be added, omitted, or altered. The oft-told Thanksgiving story of Squanto provides an excellent example for demonstrating this phenomenon. The intermediate teacher might begin this approach by reading from a contemporary textbook account such as this one:

> Samoset had returned to Plymouth with another Indian, Squanto, who could also speak English. Squanto had once lived near Plymouth Bay. He had been captured and taken to England for a short time.
>
> Squanto became a good friend to the Pilgrims. He showed them how to plant corn and other foods. He showed them how to place dead fish with the seeds to make the soil rich and the crops grow well. Squanto probably showed the Pilgrims the best ways to hunt such game as deer, rabbits, and wild turkeys.
>
> Squanto also knew where to find wild plums, strawberries, and grapes in the forest. Squanto helped the Pilgrims make friends with the other Indians. Because of Squanto, the Pilgrims learned much about how to live in America.[71]

Immediately following the reading of the contemporary textbook account, the teacher might say something like this:

> Now I am going to read to you from the *first* story of the Plymouth Colony. This was written by William Bradford, the second governor of the Plymouth Colony. Bradford has sometimes been called "the father of American history" because of his *History of Plymouth Plantation*. Most later histories about Plymouth have come from Bradford's story, including the one I just read a minute ago. Listen carefully as I read. Then we will talk about both the "old" story and the "new" one.

Next, the teacher would read passages from Bradford's account such as the following, each of which deals with Squanto:

> . . . Squanto continued with them, and was their interpreter, and was a spetiall instrument sent of God for their good beyond their expectation. He directed them how to set their corne, where to take fish, and to procure

---

[70] *Ibid.*, p. 100.

[71] O. Lawrence Burnette, Jr., and Lettie Lee Ralph, *Basic Social Studies: 5* (New York: Harper & Row, Publishers, 1964), pp. 31–32.

other commodities, and was also their pilott to bring them to unknowne places for their profitt, and never left them till he dyed. . . .

.   .   .   .

Afterwards they (as many as were able) began to plant ther corne, in which servise Squanto stood them in great stead, showing them both the maner how to set it, and after how to dress and tend it. Also he tould them excepte they gott fish and set with it (in these old grounds) it would come to nothing. . . .

.   .   .   .

. . . But upon some rumors heard, Hobamak, their Indean, tould them upon some jealocies he had, he feared they were joyned with the Narighansets and might betray them if they were not carefull. He intimated also some jealocie of Squanto, by what he gathered from some private whispering betweene him and other Indeans. But they resolved to proseede, and sente out their shalop with 10. of their cheefe men aboute the beginning of Aprill, and both Squanto and Hobamake with them, in regarde of the jelocie betweene them. . . .

.   .   .   .

. . . they begane to see that Squanto sought his owne ends, and plaid his owne game, by putting the Indeans in fear, and drawing gifts from them to enrich him selfe; making them beleeve he could stur up warr against whom he would, and make peece for whom he would. . . .[72]

The teacher could then ask his charges to identify similarities and dissimilarities in the "old" and "new" accounts and then invite them to try to explain some of the differences. The children might begin by saying that both of the stories read were about Squanto and the help he gave the Pilgrims. They might observe that the two narratives had a different "sound," and that one was easier to understand than the other. Gradually, they should point out that the "new" version added the authors' guess that Squanto might have shown the Pilgrims the best ways of hunting game, but that it left out the material in the "old" description about Squanto's jealousy and his use of others to accomplish his own purposes, and so on. In attempting to explain some of the differences, they could say that the textbook might not have had room for the whole story of Squanto; that the authors did not want to say anything unkind about this friend of the Pilgrims; and the like. The point here would not be to criticize the contemporary book or to encourage debunking but simply to help children discover that written accounts can change from time to time.

---

[72] William T. Davis (ed.), *Bradford's History of Plymouth Plantation: 1606–1646,* Vol. VI of J. Franklin Jameson (general ed.), *Original Narratives of Early American History* (New York: Charles Scribner's Sons, 1908), pp. 111, 116, 127, 128.

The fifth and final component in our series would be an examination of the ways in which the historian's perspective is influenced by the data available to him, by the clues he can uncover, and by his creative interpretation of documents, artifacts, etc., used by former peoples but unknown to his own society and culture. Innumerable examples drawn from the past which could help learners arrive at this understanding should occur readily to teachers. The assumption that the Neandertal people had some form of religion—since they buried their dead with weapons, ornaments, etc., either for use in another life or as offerings— is an hypothesis formed on the basis of known, though very limited, evidence. Theories have been and are still being developed in an endeavor to draw meaning from the remains of the Stonehenge on Salisbury Plain, in Wiltshire, England. The teacher could glean other illustrations from books like the National Geographic Society's *Everyday Life in Ancient Times.*[73] After several concrete examples have been provided and the basic point has been sufficiently established, the teacher might offer the following summary and then ask the class to respond thoughtfully and creatively to the fictional situation outlined below:

> We have seen how historians and others have used many things left by past peoples to try to put together stories about life long ago. We have said that it is very hard for a person to get all of the information he would like to have about some earlier civilizations. We have noticed that sometimes a person can only make a careful guess about the things others before him thought, and felt, and did. We have said that a person understands his own way of life best because it is closest to him. And we have found out that a person often tries to explain things he does not understand from the past by making them fit things he does understand in the present.
>
> Now, let's see how well your imaginations are working today! Let's pretend that a new school is going to be built in our city. It has been decided that there will be a big cornerstone ceremony with the Superintendent of Schools and many others attending. The Superintendent of Schools wants a group of children to choose some things that will be cemented behind the cornerstone. The things the children choose should tell important parts of the story of their way of life to someone living many, many, many years from now who might find these things and might want to write about the people who left them there.
>
> Let's imagine that all of the children in our class have been asked to do the choosing. What would you choose, and why?
>
> I have some 3″ x 5″ cards here. I will give each one of you five cards at first. If you want more cards, you may come up to my desk and

---

[73] Washington, D.C.: National Geographic Society, 1958.

get them. Put one thing you think should be included on each card. In a little bit, we will make a list on the board of all of your ideas. Then, we will talk about each thing and see whether it is a good choice. Finally, we will try to imagine the problems someone might have five hundred or a thousand years from now if he tried to describe *our* way of life by examining the "clues" you decided to leave in the cornerstone.

CONCLUSION

> Life—with its endless possibilities, and its unique
> present which never happens twice.
> DAG HAMMARSKJOLD

Walter Sellar and Robert Yeatman, in their droll and whimsical little book *1066 and All That,* warn the reader that theirs is a *"memorable history of England, comprising all the parts you can remember, including one hundred and three good things, five bad kings, and two genuine dates."* [74] There is an element of truth in their notion of what it is that people remember from their exposure to history as a school subject. We hope this volume has helped the reader—whether layman or professional educator—to range far beyond this narrow concept. If this book has served its purpose, the reader will have become more aware of the value, significance, and dynamism of history as an academic discipline. He will see (and, if he is a teacher, he will help his students see) the relentlessness of change. He will better understand the complexity of the task of the historian as he goes about the job of ordering the past, as well as developing the invaluable habit of seeing the past through the eyes of those who lived it. Perhaps the perceptive reader will also come away from his experience with this book with a more realistic understanding of the "uses of the past." He will have learned something of history's promise and something of its limitations, as well as an appreciation of the incalculable debt modern man owes to those who preceded him.

Crane Brinton once said that "all normal people . . . have some desire to locate themselves in a 'system,' a 'universe,' a 'process' transcending at least the immediate give and take between the individual and his environment." [75] We are certain that children share this desire to see themselves in some sort of historical perspective, to see themselves as part of something more than a given moment in time. This natural wish, combined with the insights presented by Professor Commager and

---

[74] New York: E. P. Dutton & Co., Inc., 1931, title page.
[75] Crane Brinton, *op. cit.,* p. 11.

the techniques described by the editors, ought to result in a broader, more mature, and more functional understanding of history. Teachers, having expanded their understanding of history's assets and liabilities, may become less dogmatic and more likely to recognize Mueller's warning that "in the final analysis there can be no final analysis"—more likely, in short, to bring more of the historian's brand of history into the classroom.

Perhaps the prophetic H. G. Wells has given us the most fitting insight with which to end this volume. In his *The Discovery of the Future,* he looks both backward and forward in time, and concludes that

> The past is but the beginning of a beginning, and all that is and has been is but the twilight of the dawn. . . . A day will come when beings who are now latent in our thoughts and hidden in our loins shall stand upon this earth as one stands upon a footstool, and shall laugh and reach out their hands amid the stars.[76]

---

[76] In *Annual Report of the Board of Regents of the Smithsonian Institution* (Washington: Government Printing Office, 1903), p. 392.

INDEX

Index

Acton, Lord, qt. 25, 54, 55; on moral judgment, 63
Adams, Henry, qt. 43, 61, 82, 84
Adams, John, literature on, 32

Beard, Charles A., qt. 48, 53; on judgment in history, 64
Becker, Carl L., 15
Berlin, Isaiah, qt. 65
Biography, in history, 82
Bolingbroke, Lord, 61, 91
Bossuet, Jacques, 80
Brooks, Van Wyck, qt. 9, 41
Burckhardt, Jacob, qt. 1
Butterfield, Herbert, qt. 10, 13, 69

Carlyle, Thomas, qt. 24, 77
Carr, E. H., qt. 68
Causation in history, 79 ff.
Chance, in history, 85–88
Character, in history, 93–94
Cheyney, Edward P., on laws in history, 84
Chronology, problems of, 16 ff.
Churchill, Winston S., 91, 94
Civil War, literature of, 30–31
Constitution, federal, literature on, 33, 50
Croce, Benedetto, 1, qt. 71
Cultural history, 20–22; anthropology, 22–24

Declaration of Independence, 50
Documents, in history, 50

Eliot, George, qt. 88
Emerson, R. W., qt. 78

Facts, in history, 48 ff.
Fiction, historical, 34–36
Fisher, H. A. L., qt. 85
Fiske, John, qt. 83

Florence, described, 75
Force, in history, 81
Fortuity, in history, 85–88
Freeman, Douglas S., 30, 57
Freeman, Edward A., qt. 20
Froude, James A., qt. 62

Geography, and history, 18
Greek Anthology, qt. 53

Harrison, Frederic, qt. 2
Hawthorne, Nathaniel, 76
Hazard, Paul, qt. 57
Herodotus, qt. 66
Historical fiction, 34–36
Historical writing, biography, 39–40, 82
Historicism, 57, 61
History, as memory, 2; as story, 3; as record, 3–6; interpretation of, 6; as literature, 6–8; as science, 9–11, 12–13; as philosophy, 11; contemporary, 18; patterns of, 18; as biography, 24 ff.; what to read, 27 ff.; geography and exploration, 28; writing of, 37 ff.; writing, choice of subject, 38–40; style, 41; limitations on, 44; patterns of, national, 46; periodization, 46; bias, 54; interpretation of, 54 ff.; subjectivity of, 55; judgment in, 60 ff.; imagination in, 77–78; causation in, 79 ff.; fortuity in, 85–88; uses of, 92.
Holmes, Justice O. W., qt. 66

Imagination in history, 38
Inevitability, doctrine of, 47–48

James, Henry, qt. 75
Jefferson, Thomas, literature on, 31–32

Johnson, Edward, 80
Judgment, in history, 60 ff.;
    professional, 65, 71

Law in history, 83 ff.
Lincoln, Abraham, qt. 67
Leutze, Emanuel, 51

Macaulay, Lord, qt. 3, 74
Madison's *Notes,* as history, 1–2
Maitland, Frederic, qt. 46
Matthiessen, Francis, qt. 10
Moody, William Vaughn, qt. 52
Moral judgment in history, 60 ff.
Motley, John L., qt. 62–3

Namier, Lewis, 26
National character, 22–23
Nationalism, in history, 55 ff.
Note-taking, problem of, 40 ff.
Nevins, Allan, qt. 7
Newtonian history, 81

Panofsky, Edwin, 51
Parker, Theodore, qt. 57
Parkman, Francis, qt. 7
Phillip II of Spain, 62
Philosophy in history, 72 ff.; of
    history, 89 ff.

Plato, qt. 66
Political history, 19
Poussin, painting, 61
Present-mindedness, 46
Progress, doctrine of, 82

Raleigh, Walter, qt. 91
Reconstruction, in United States,
    interpretation of, 59

St. Augustine, qt. 80
Salem, Massachusetts, described, 76
Schlesinger, Arthur S., Jr., qt. 6, 88
Slavery, judgment on, 67
Socrates, qt. 60
Spencer, Herbert, qt. 83
Spender, Stephen, qt. 30

"Technical" history, 13
Toynbee, Arnold, 64
Treitschke, Heinrich von, 53
Trevelyan, George M., qt. 10, 74,
    77, 90

Voltaire, Francois, qt. 90

Wedgwood, Veronica, qt. 43, 64
Woolf, Virginia, qt. 14
Wordsworth, William, qt. 29, 72